Distinguished Studies in

American Legal and Constitutional History

Harold M. Hyman, General Editor
William P. Hobby Professor of History
Rice University

A Garland Series

FRONTISPIECE. Holmes portrait upon receiving Honorary Doctorate from Oxford, Summer, 1909. *Harvard Law School Art Collection.*

Justice Holmes and the Natural Law

by

Michael H. Hoffheimer

Garland Publishing, Inc.
New York & London 1992

Library of Congress Cataloging-in-Publication Data

Hoffheimer, Michael H., 1954–
Justice Holmes and the natural law / by Michael H. Hoffheimer.
p. cm. — (Distinguished studies in American legal and constitutional history)
Includes bibliographical references and index.
ISBN 0–8153–0896–5
1. Holmes, Oliver Wendell, 1841–1935—Views on natural law.
2. Natural law. I. Title. II. Series.
K474.H632H63 1992
340'.112—dc20 92–24771
CIP

All volumes printed on acid-free, 250-year-life paper
Manufactured in the United States of America

Designed by Kathryn Semble

For
my father
Harry M. Hoffheimer

Contents

List of Illustrations

Preface

THIS BOOK is not intended as a new biography of Justice Oliver Wendell Holmes or as a critical study of his legal philosophy. Rather, it is intended to help fill a gap in the studies of Holmes. Without denying the power with which Holmes reacted against intellectual traditions of the nineteenth century, I hope to show that natural law and transcendentalist philosophy formed important vital sources of his mature legal theory.

Appreciating the continuity of transcendentalist and natural law influences contributes to a more complete, sympathetic, and accurate reconstruction of Holmes's philosophy of law. And by helping place Holmes in historical context, I hope to contribute to an understanding of pervasive continuities in nineteenth- and early twentieth-century thought.

Since starting my work on Holmes I have witnessed the publication of several pounds of new scholarship on him. This has made me mindful of Ibn Khaldun's observation in 1377 that "among the things that are harmful to the human quest for knowledge and to the attainment of a thorough scholarship are the great number of works available."[1] Holmes's own writings remain a rewarding starting point for historical knowledge, and they are readily accessible. It would be sad if the growth of scholarship on Holmes led to a decline of interest in his work itself. One of my goals has been to awaken interest in some of his early writings, which often have been overlooked. They are reprinted here in their entirety as appendices.

I have tried to be brief. If reducing some arguments has endangered clarity, the alternative seemed worse. My argument and interpretation are supported by conventional pre-postmodern approaches to intellectual history. I have tried to avoid creating the illusion that I am the source of this story, the features and sources of which are familiar to most students of Holmes. And I have tried to avoid giving any impression that my description or explanation is exhaustive. An occasional allusion (such as the title's resonance with myth in Chapter 3) is meant as invitation, not direction.

---

[1] I. Khaldun, *The Muquddimah: An Introduction to History* 414 (F. Rosenthal trans. N. Dawood ed. 1967).

The chapters address distinct problems that are posed by Holmes's intellectual biography, and they employ significantly different methods. It may be helpful to summarize the argument at the beginning.

Chapter 1 discusses scholarly attention to the Holmes "problem." I argue that most treatments of tension or conflict in Holmes are incomplete because they assume that he consistently rejected natural law and idealist philosophy. I suggest, in contrast, that his ambivalent relation to natural law and idealist philosophy provided an important source of tension in his theory—tension that illuminates the origins of his legal theory and its pivotal role in the history of modern American legal thought.

Chapter 2 treats Holmes's early philosophical ideas. In investigating his college writings, I try to show that he had fully assimilated transcendentalist philosophy and had become an original, serious proponent of an extreme form of philosophical idealism. Though he was familiar with positivist thinkers and incorporated some of their arguments, he did not understand the new theory as incompatible with the idealist views he championed. At the same time, his idealist theory of history and art resulted in an intellectual impasse.

Chapter 3 addresses biographical problems presented by Holmes's intellectual development. Applying an explicitly psychological framework, I question the accuracy of Holmes's autobiographical statements about his formative influences. Considering his troubled relation with his father, I suggest that Holmes's mature legal theory evinces a concern with control of conflict that reflected an internalization and intellectualization of conflict. I try to show that the emotional force behind his criticism of idealism and natural law manifested biographical origins of his concern with conflict. But I try to show also that his legal philosophy never fully eliminated important features of natural law and idealism. Conflict and control provided mechanics for a conception of law and a model of legal theory that remained deeply touched by the human goals and spiritual aspirations that derived from the traditions of transcendentalism and natural law.

Oxford, Mississippi
July 1, 1992

Acknowledgments

THE SCHOLARSHIP on Justice Oliver Wendell Holmes is remarkable for its high quality, and it is impossible to acknowledge all of my intellectual debts. The influence of the scholarship of Mark DeWolfe Howe and G. Edward White in particular cannot be fully expressed by my many notes to their work.

I have received much personal help, which improved my understanding of Holmes and made the study of Holmes a pleasure. Robert Stoddart provided expert help with Greek, and I am very grateful for his willingness to translate the Greek prize essay (Appendix B). I received advice, criticism, and encouragement from Luanne Buchanan, Larry S. Bush, Michael H. Cardozo, Peter Gay, Thomas A. Green, Robert J. Hawes, Daniel J. Hoffheimer, Harry M. Hoffheimer, James L. Robertson, Andrew S. Watson, G. Edward White, and Philip P. Wiener. I received bibliographic help from Mrs. James H. Chadbourn, Herbert E. Cihak, J. Wesley Cochran, Judith Mellins, and the late Ellis Tucker.

Research was funded by grants from the Lamar Order, University of Mississippi Law School. I am grateful to the law school, its alumni, and my colleagues for their support and interest.

The following institutions granted permission to publish copies of material from their collections: Harvard Law School Library, Harvard University Archives, Houghton Library, Supreme Court Historical Society, and the Museum of Fine Arts, Boston.

Justice Holmes and the Natural Law

CHAPTER 1

Problems with the Holmes Problem

THE SCHOLARSHIP on Justice Oliver Wendell Holmes was marked by polemic long before his death. Conflicting judgments about the merit of his opinions mirrored conflicting interpretations of the content of his thought.[1] Holmes scholars, reflecting on the polemical character of Holmes studies and self-conscious of changes in his posthumous reputation, have come to recognize important tensions and conflicts within his thought itself. Recent biographers agree that Holmes's life and thought were signally conflicted. One biographer describes the contradictory interpretations of Holmes and suggests that "[i]t is not possible to reduce his work to any one system."[2] Another biographer depicts Holmes as enigma.[3] Still another biographer reasserts the provocative claim that, beneath his liberal facade, Holmes embraced "a kind of fascist ideology."[4]

Friends tolerated the contradictions[5] while critics exploited them. Lon Fuller charged that "Holmes' case suggests furthermore that the positivistic attitude may often represent the emotional resolution of a

---

[1]The history of Holmes's reputation is discussed in White, *Looking at Holmes in the Mirror*, 4 *Law & Hist. Rev.* 439 (1986); White, *The Rise and Fall of Justice Holmes*, 39 *U. Chi. L. Rev.* 51, 53 (1971).

[2]L. Baker, *The Justice From Beacon Hill: The Life and Times of Oliver Wendell Holmes* 11 (1991).

[3]G. Aichele, *Oliver Wendell Holmes, Jr.: Soldier, Scholar, Judge* ix (1989), writes: "[I]t is difficult to study the life and work of Oliver Wendell Holmes, Jr., for very long without becoming uncomfortably aware of the enigmatic nature of this seminal figure in American legal history."

[4]S. Novick, *Honorable Justice: The Life of Oliver Wendell Holmes* xvii (1989). *See also id.* at 351, 445, 478. *But see* White, *Holmes's "Life Plan": Confronting Ambition, Passion, and Powerlessness*, 65 *N.Y.U.L. Rev.* 1409, 1416 (1990) (Novick's controversial assertions are not documented).

Novick's biography contains a good bibliography of Holmes's writings. S. Novick, *supra*, at 400–07. Its omission of published correspondence is corrected by Thomson, *Playing with a Mirage: Oliver Wendell Holmes, Jr. and American Law*, 22 *Rutgers L. J.* 123, 168–71 (1990).

[5]At the celebration of Holmes's ninetieth birthday, Chief Justice Hughes characterized him as a "constant contradiction of all that great age usually implies." Quoted in L. Baker, *supra* note 2, at 3.

conflict between the opposing forces of romanticism and skepticism at war in the same breast."[6] By emphasizing important inconsistencies, critics sought to debunk liberal interpretations of Holmes. His celebrated opinions that defended individual liberties[7] were incompatible with other opinions that authorized seemingly unlimited government interference with such liberties.[8] Mencken observed with cynicism that Holmes's dissents in support of social welfare legislation[9] expressed his judicial concern less for rights of individuals than for "rights of lawmakers."[10]

Attacks on Holmes's liberal reputation continue. Recent studies have also found internal inconsistency within opinions deferring to state legislative authority[11] and within opinions treating first amendment rights.[12]

Despite widespread recognition of tensions in Holmes's thought, most interpreters have dismissed the tensions as simple inconsistencies.[13] A few writers have seized on the tensions as

---

[6]*E.g.*, L. Fuller, *The Law in Quest of Itself* 107 (1940). *See also* Boorstin, *The Elusiveness of Mr. Justice Holmes*, 14 *The New England Q.* 478, 485 (1941); D. Burton, *Oliver Wendel Holmes, Jr.* 89 (1980).

[7]*E.g.*, Gitlow v. New York, 268 U.S. 652 (1925) (Holmes, J., dissenting); Abrams v. United States, 250 U.S. 616 (1919) (Holmes, J., dissenting).

[8]*E.g.*, Buck v. Bell, 274 U.S. 200 (1927) (Holmes, J.).

[9]*E.g.*, Lochner v. New York, 198 U.S. 45 (1905) (Holmes, J., dissenting).

[10]Mencken, *Mr. Justice Holmes*, in H. Mencken, *The Vintage Mencken* 190 (A. Cooke comp. 1955). Mencken anticipated a school of Holmes criticism in arguing that the central principle of Holmes's philosophy of law was a policy of judicial deference to legislative power. Mencken acknowledged the existence of a few opinions that defended individual liberty interests but explained them as the result of inconsistency. *Id.* at 191–92.

[11]*See* Roberts, *Mining with Mr. Justice Holmes*, 39 *Vand. L. Rev.* 287, 292 (1986) (suggesting possible inconsistency in Holmes's rejection of substantive due process limitations in takings cases but dismissing the suggestion as improbable).

[12]*See* Hunter, *Problems in Search of Principles: The First Amendment in the Supreme Court from 1791–1930*, 35 *Emory L.J.* 59, 107 (1986) (illustrating inconsistency in Holmes's treatment of First Amendment cases); Robban, *The Emergence of Modern First Amendment Doctrine*, 50 *U. Chi. L. Rev.* 1205, 1303–27 (1983) (discussing Holmes's impact on development of modern first amendment analysis).

[13]White argues that Holmes's professional career reflected a highly self-conscious "life plan" that reflected his response to a need to contain passion (including but not limited to romantic passion) and a sense of vulnerability that he suffered throughout his adult life. His friendships and his speeches thus appear as searches for intimacy and an escape from routine. White goes far toward explaining differences in mood, tone, and even personality that are revealed in different facets of Holmes's life, and White demonstrates that they are closely interrelated. *See generally* White, *Holmes's "Life Plan":*

evidence that Holmes lacked any coherent intellectual position at all.[14] Ironically, one reason for the neglect of central tensions in Holmes is that most have taken Holmes at his word when he attacked transcendental theories of natural law. Holmes remains considered almost universally as a utilitarian, positivist, pragmatist, or realist in his basic theory, despite the fact that sensitive scholars applying the labels have recognized the inconsistency that results from their application.

The tensions within Holmes's theoretical writings are not superficial. They touch on his conception of the nature of law itself. His great book *The Common Law* (1881) demonstrated how law evolved by means of internal organic rules that led to the law's becoming increasingly objective and aware of its own mission.[15] In keeping with the vision of *The Common Law*, the lawyer's task as part of the historical process was to participate actively in freeing the law from those archaic doctrines that prevented the law from consciously fulfilling its role of promoting social policy. Yet his later work *The Path of the Law* (1897) treated the law as the prediction of the outcome of future judicial decisions. The vision of the later work reduced the lawyer's task to accurate prediction. The different works did not just employ two different meanings of the word "law." They emphasized two different visions of the role of law in society, of the role of the lawyer in the practice of law, and of the ends toward which legal change ran.[16]

Confronting Ambition, Passion, and Powerlessness, 65 *N.Y.U.L. Rev.* 1409 (1990). For a compelling reconstruction of the persona that emerges in Holmes's activity as a correspondent, *see* White, *Holmes as Correspondent*, 43 *Vand. L. Rev.* 1717, 1757–61 (1990).

[14]*See* L. Baker, *supra* note 2, at 11; Gordon, *Holmes' Common Law as Legal and Social Science*, 10 *Hofstra L. Rev.* 719, 722 (1982).

[15]Grey emphasizes that Holmes rejected a logical—formal and articulate—expression of the common law in the work. Grey, *Holmes and Legal Pragmatism*, 41 *Stanford L. Rev.* 787, 816 (1989). It is true that the book's descriptive, historical, and analytic treatment of common law rejected the possibility of a logical retroactive exposition. But the thread of the analysis was pulled by a prescriptive vision of the growth of an ever more rational expression of the law. The growing rationality was expressed both in a tighter fit between legal rule and social polity and by increased coherence. The latter was manifested by externalization or objectification of standards *and* by the ability of appellate courts (or their predictors) to articulate the rule, and thus to apply the rule uniformly.

[16]There is a shift of emphasis from the historical exposition of law in 1880 to the return to a practical, predictive definition in *The Path of the Law*. Much of the scholarship that addresses inconsistencies in Holmes's writings has oddly avoided the most obvious explanation—namely, that his views did change in important respects. Some of the striking differences between *The*

Holmes has been different things to different generations. To the present generation of legal scholars he represents a *problem* that needs to be pursued,[17] interpreted, or simply exposed.[18] Notwithstanding the growing self-reflective character of contemporary scholarship on Holmes and the recognition of important tensions in his work, his ideas are still usually explained in terms that scholars proposed earlier this century and that became fixed within a decade after his death.[19]

Common Law and *The Path of the Law* are certainly illuminated by considering Holmes's biography. The scholar-lawyer protagonist of historical progress in *The Common Law* reflected Holmes's activity and aspirations at the time he wrote it. The importance of predicting future decisions of appellate courts manifested in *The Path of the Law* revealed its author's concern as an appellate judge and, perhaps, as White suggests, Holmes's growing appreciation of the limits of judicial power outside the courtroom. White, *Holmes's "Life Plan": Confronting Ambition, Passion, and Powerlessness*, *supra* note 13, at 1477 ("[T]he evolution of his conception of law . . . can be seen as a progressive recognition that the course and content of law is being driven not by Holmes, the systematic thinker, but by the infamous 'bad man' who plays no part in formulating legal thought."); White, *The Integrity of Holmes' Jurisprudence*, 10 *Hofstra L. Rev.* 633, 650–51 (1982).

The predictive theory of law was not new, however, for Holmes had proposed a predictive definition of law during his lectures at Harvard years before *The Common Law*. He referred to his own views in the July 1872 issue of *The American Law Review*:

> In the lectures . . . it was doubted whether law, in the more limited meaning which lawyers give to the word, possessed any other common attribute than of being enforced by the procedure of the courts, and therefore of practical importance to lawyers.

Book Notice, 6 *Am. L. Rev.* 723 (1872), reprinted in O. Holmes, *The Formative Essays of Justice Holmes: The Making of an American Legal Philosophy* 91 (F. Kellogg ed. 1984). *See also id.* at 92 ("The only question for the lawyer is, how will the judges act?").

[17]Thomson writes of the "searching" for Holmes and the "surfeit of commentary" that has resulted. His judgment as to the likelihood of finding Holmes may be reflected in the title of his study, Thomson, *supra* note 4, at 125–26. Aichele, too, alludes to the illusory object of the biographer's quest: "In the end, the figure that emerges will be seen from the perspective of the present age, and not in the light of his own." G. Aichele, *supra* note 3, at xi. He passes the task of ultimate judgment to the reader. *Id.* at xi, 166.

[18]*E.g.*, Gordon, *supra* note 14, at 722; Note, *Holmes: A Legend in Search of Demystification*, 103 *Harv. L. Rev.* 800 (1990).

[19]The interpretation of Holmes as positivist, pragmatist, utilitarian, or realist was shared by Holmes's friends and foes alike. *See, e.g.*, L. Fuller, *supra* note 6, at 62, 106–07 (describing Holmes as realist and positivist);

A. Scholarly Assumptions

Debate continues about the appropriate classification of Holmes as positivist or pragmatist or realist or utilitarian.[20] Of course, the literature on Holmes is so vast that it includes a few oddities. One writer in 1937 claimed that Holmes was a mystic.[21] But most scholars ignored such oddities, and few serious students of Holmes have doubted that he was at bottom an advocate of an extreme sort of instrumental legal philosophy. Nor have they questioned the concomitant biographical assumption that the main sources and inspirations for his work were nineteenth-century English and American analytic philosophers—with a little Comte stirred in—and writers from the German Historical School.

Prevailing interpretations of Holmes disagree in their evaluation of his coherence, originality, and worth. But they share an important assumption about what Holmes was not. They agree implicitly that he was not a proponent of natural law in any form. They assume that continental rationalist and idealist strains of thought—and American proponents like Emerson—had no important influence on the mature theory of Holmes. So, too, the literature reflects the historical assumption that Holmes's mature philosophy marked a radical break with the philosophy of law current at the end of the eighteenth century. And it assumes his own intellectual development was achieved by a radical break with the transcendentalist views that he held in his early adulthood.

The assumption of radical discontinuity is troublesome, however, for the evidence is weak. Indeed, the reasoning behind the

---

Howe, *The Positivism of Mr. Justice Holmes*, 64 *Harv. L. Rev.* 529 (1923) (describing Holmes as positivist).

[20]Grey characterizes Holmes as a pragmatist and seeks the source of apparent inconsistency in conflict between his theory and historical, personal, and other factors that prevented him from implementing the theory consistently. Grey, *supra*, note 15, at 788. Pohlman claims Holmes for the analytic utilitarian tradition in English language philosophy. H.L. Pohlman, *Justice Oliver Wendell Holmes: Utilitarian Jurisprudence* 1–10 (1984). Gordon and Kelley reject the characterization of Holmes as a pragmatist and class him as a positivist. Gordon, *supra* note 14, at 721–23; Kelley, *Was Holmes a Pragmatist? Reflections on a new Twist to an Old Argument*, 14 *Sou. Ill. U.L.J.* 427, 467 (1990); Kelley, *Book Review*, 68 *Wash. U.L.Q.* 429 452 (1990).

[21]"Among the moderns, no one can be classified more assuredly among the elect than our own Emerson. . . . In close intellectual affinity and spiritual kinship with the band of the 'chosen people,' I place Holmes, jurist and philosopher." G. Farnum, *Holmes the Mystic Philosopher* n.p. (1937), *reprinted from The Lawyer* (1937). I discuss the views of Wu in the Epilogue.

assumption rests on a circular argument.[22] Interpretation of Holmes's ideas as a radical innovation became a standard part of legal historiography,[23] but that historiography itself rested on a sort of circular argument if Holmes's intellectual biography did not provide concrete evidence of innovation. The historical assumptions evade rather than confront what should be central topics in modern legal history and in Holmes's personal history.

The scholarly insistence upon Holmes's originality has tended to obscure the contribution of natural law to modern legal thought. Holmes's earliest criticism of legal doctrines associated with natural law actually advanced the rather limited argument that duty preceded right—logically and historically. He supported the argument with a sociological and instrumental explanation of sovereignty.[24] But few scholars have examined the specific features of natural law doctrine that Holmes rejected. Natural law itself has usually not even been defined but has been understood to be the theory that there is some superlaw that exists independently of any law that is the product of a real jurisdiction's legal system. But this conception of natural law as superlaw that informs the views of its critics is questionable.[25]

The prevailing assumption that natural law theory represented a metaphysical confusion of law and morals and resorted to the supersensible has obscured the origins of Holmes's views on the important problem of the relation of law and "science." The neglect of natural law is bound up with the assumption that the movement for legal "science" was inspired by positivism or, perhaps, the Historical

---

[22]Pohlman makes the same point in arguing that Holmes was a utilitarian. H. Pohlman, *supra* note 20, at 3.

[23]Writers continue to protest against the undue emphasis on Holmes's novelty and originality. *See* LaPiana, *Victorian from Beacon Hill: Oliver Wendell Holmes's Early Legal Scholarship*, 90 *Columbia L. Rev.* 809 (1990), but the general reaction against Holmes that began almost a generation ago has now filtered into popular treatments. The narrative monographs of Kermit Hall and Lawrence Friedmann pointedly ignore giving prominent treatment to Holmes.

[24]*See generally* Holmes, *Codes, and the Arrangement of the Law*, 5 *Am. L. Rev.* 1 (1870), *reprinted in* O. Holmes, *The Formative Essays, supra* note 16.

[25]The definition of natural law as belief in a superlaw is tendentious: it is doubtful whether important proponents of natural law adhered to the doctrine as it has been defined by their critics. Roscoe Pound, who viewed natural law sympathetically and who continued to take it more seriously than most of his contemporaries, explained natural law in historical terms as the "juristic idealization of the social order of the time and place." R. Pound, *Interpretations of Legal History* 5 (1923) (1986 reprint).

School.[26] But the distinction between legal science and moral philosophy did not first emerge in nineteenth-century writings but rather in the works of eighteenth-century idealist philosophers.[27] And Holmes did not get the idea of a *science* of law from either Maine or the positivists. The idea of "science" had attained currency a generation earlier in the writings of natural law theorists. For example, Joseph Story had referred repeatedly to law as "science" a generation before Holmes.[28] Commitment to natural law principles did not prevent Story from likening legal science to the natural sciences. Developments in both law and science supported Story's vision of progress transcending limitations and moving toward an absolute:

> In truth, the common law, as a science, must be forever in progress; and no limits can be assigned to its principles or improvements. In this respect it resembles the natural sciences, where new discoveries continually lead the way to new, and sometimes to astonishing, results. . . . It is its true glory, that it is flexible, and constantly expanding with the exigencies of society; that it daily presents new motives for new and loftier efforts; that it holds out forever an unapproached degree of excellence; that it moves onward in the path towards perfection, but never arrives at the ultimate point.[29]

The association of legal "science" with natural law rather than with positivism or formalism seemingly accounts for Holmes's emphatic

---

[26]*E.g.*, LaPiana, *supra* note 23, at 810–18 (explaining Holmes as part of a movement for a "new legal science" that appeared mid-century); Kelley, *Was Holmes a Pragmatist? supra* note 20, at 460–62 (emphasizing the positivist influence upon Holmes's effort to introduce scientific principles into law); Touster, *Holmes a Hundred Years Ago: "The Common Law" and Legal Theory*, 10 *Hofstra L. Rev.* 673, 685 (1982) (emphasizing the influence of Maine and the Historical School and describing Holmes's work as "*scientific* in the broadest sense").

[27]German "legal science" is today associated with followers of the Historical School. *See generally* Reimann, *Nineteenth-Century German Legal Science* 31 *Boston C. L. Rev.* 837, 851 (1990), but Kant and his idealist successors, Schelling and Hegel, had earlier insisted on the distinction between the science of moral philosophy and legal science. *See* Hoffheimer, *Schelling's Philosophy of Natural Law*, 64 *Temple L. Rev.* 1 (1991).

[28]*See, e.g.*, *Speech at the Centennial Celebration of Harvard University*, in *The Miscellaneous Writings of Joseph Story* 737 (W. Story ed. 1852) (1972 reprint): "No one appreciates more fully than myself the general importance of the study of the law. No one places a higher value on that science." *See also Course of Legal Study* (1817), in *id.* at 66, 69–70, 84.

[29]*Value and Importance of Legal Studies* (1829), in *id.* at 526.

remark, "Law is not a science, but is essentially empirical."[30] Yet his systematic and historical defense of judicial lawmaking in *The Common Law* expressed a progressive understanding of the common law that was far more compatible with Story than with Austin.

Nineteenth-century natural law writings displayed characteristic doctrines and attitudes that anticipated important, distinctive features of the mature legal philosophy of Holmes. Holmes's failure to acknowledge the influence of transcendentalism or natural law on his legal theory poses a difficulty that is not different in kind from his failure to admit the influence of pragmatism or utilitarianism, which were powerful sources of his ideas.[31]

His failure to acknowledge the effect of natural law and idealist philosophy contrasts with the appreciation of these sources by other legal writers in the half-century after the Civil War. Founders of the new American science of law often acknowledged a debt to natural law theory and idealist philosophy. Sheldon Amos wrote that "Modern Jurisprudence is emphatically a German creation," and he acknowledged the Historical School, and also Kant and Hegel, among his intellectual progenitors.[32] Roscoe Pound observed that nineteenth-century education was less influenced by English political writers than by natural law juristic writers and by continental philosophers permeated with Hegelian views.[33]

---

[30] *Codes, and the Arrangement of the Law*, in O. Holmes, *The Formative Essays*, *supra* note 24, at 80.

[31] Grey points out that Holmes repeatedly criticized William James and claimed that he rejected pragmatism; Grey further questions the motive and validity of the exception, where Holmes expressed admiration for Dewey. This evidence did not prevent Grey from arguing plausibly that Holmes was a pragmatist. Grey, *supra* note 15, at 864–70 (appendix on Holmes and the Pragmatists). Pohlman's entire argument for a utilitarian influence on Holmes is based on interpretation of internal evidence, and he quickly dismisses Holmes's expressed criticism of proponents of utilitarian legal theory: "Of course Holmes considered himself a critic of Austin and Bentham. But we cannot grant Holmes the privilege of writing his own intellectual biography." H. Pohlman, *supra* note 20, at 4.

Holmes's reluctance to accept intellectual influences is an important biographical phenomenon and is addressed in Chapter 3.

[32] S. Amos, *The Science of Jurisprudence* 505 (1872), *quoted in* Reimann, *supra* note 27, 837.

[33] *See* R. Pound, *The Revival of Natural Law*, 17 *Notre Dame L. Rev.* 287, 333 (1942).

B. Holmes's Critique of Natural Law

Holmes did not just refuse to acknowledge the influence of natural law; he attacked natural law jurisprudence repeatedly and effectively. The widespread assumption that Holmes stood in direct opposition to natural law is supported by ample evidence. His antipathy to natural law is well documented. His intellectual activity contributed to the decline of natural law theory in this century.

Criticism of natural law occupied a special place in Holmes's theoretical iconoclasm. He brought together many of his arguments against natural law in an essay entitled *Natural Law*. Written in 1918 when Holmes was 77, the short essay was published in the *Harvard Law Review*.[34] It was one of the most forceful restatements of basic convictions that Holmes had attempted in decades.[35]

The article *Natural Law* has not attracted much scholarly attention. It did not present any new arguments, and it is largely of literary and rhetorical interest. It reaffirmed broad features of Holmes's world view that were known from other writings and speeches. In fact, the narrator repeatedly cited himself: "I used to say. . . . If, as I have suggested elsewhere. . . . If I may quote myself again. . . ."[36] The essay resonated with phrases familiar from his articles, speeches, and opinions. Notwithstanding its avowed lack of novelty, *Natural Law* set forth the basic tenets of Holmes's legal philosophy with an art and emotional power that he rarely equaled. Laski, for one, recognized the extraordinary appeal of the essay.[37]

There is reason to suspect that Holmes meant *Natural Law* as his last major writing. After finishing the article, the only other important publishing project that Holmes pursued was the edition of his *Collected Legal Papers* (1921). Holmes had probably been

---

[34]*Natural Law*, in O. Holmes, *Collected Legal Papers* 310–16 (1921). *Natural Law* was originally published as an article in 32 *Harv. L. Rev.* 40 (1918).

[35]There is a silence of a decade following the intimate expressions of his views in the speech on John Marshall (1901) and the address at the dedication of Northwestern in (1902). In 1911 Holmes began a series of short, artful expressions of his views: *The Class of '61* (1911 speech), *Reflections on the Past and Future* (1912 speech), *Law and the Court* (1913 speech), Introduction to a series on European Legal History (1913), *Ideals and Doubts*, 10 *Ill. L. Rev.* (1915).

[36]*Natural Law*, in O. Holmes, *Collected Legal Papers, supra* note 34, at 310–11.

[37]1 *Holmes-Laski Letters: The Correspondence of Mr. Justice Holmes and Harold J. Laski 1916–1935* 163, 173 (M. Howe ed. 1953).

contemplating a collection of his shorter writings for years,[38] and he took an active interest in the book.[39] Because the essays were printed in chronological order, *Natural Law* appeared in it as Holmes's last word. The essay was a work of closure, the *finis* to the compilation of articles from 1885 to 1918.

The voice of the writer of *Natural Law* wore its age with pride but emphasized that the repudiation of natural law was a conviction that ran back to his youth: "I used to say, when I was young, that truth was the majority vote of that nation that could lick all others."[40] The essay had an oral, homiletic feel. It digressed, stammered, and paused. Working itself up to emotional summary, it terminated themes with abrupt non sequiturs. Its evocative footnoteless prose[41] deviated from the stultifying conventions of law review publishing and regressed to the epigrammatic and elliptical style of Emerson.

> [F]or legal purposes a right is only the hypostasis of a prophecy—the imagination of a substance supporting the fact that the public force will be brought to bear upon those who do things said to contravene it—just as we talk of the force of gravitation accounting for the conduct of bodies in space. One phrase adds no more than the other to what we know without it. No doubt behind these legal rights is the fighting will of the subject to maintain them, and the spread of his emotions to the general rules by which they are maintained; but that does not seem to me the same thing as the supposed *a priori* discernment of a duty or the assertion of a preexisting legal right. A dog will fight for his bone.[42]

The article began by confessing the futility of engaging in philosophical debate: "Deep-seated preference can not be argued

---

[38]When Holmes discussed and later corresponded with Laski about the book, it was obvious that he had given its contents a great deal of thought. And he had himself collected copies of his articles over the years, which he had compiled in two volumes, which he offered "unwillingly" to forward to Laski. *See* letter to Laski of October 16, 1919, *id.* at 215.

[39]Laski took administrative editorial responsibility, and Holmes acknowledged his role in the Preface, but Laski was appropriately not identified as editor of the work because Holmes probably decided the contents and arrangement of the volume. The surviving correspondence with Laski reveals that Holmes persisted in pursuing the project and also reveals Holmes's interest in details of the project.

[40]*Natural Law*, in O. Holmes, *Collected Legal Papers*, *supra* note 34, at 40–44.

[41]The only footnote in the work identified a work by Francois Geny as inspiration for the essay. It was added at Laski's suggestion.

[42]*Natural Law*, in O. Holmes, *Collected Legal Papers, supra* note 34, at 315.

about—you can not argue a man into liking a glass of beer. . .,"[43] and then, by a wonderful maneuver, Holmes accused natural law theorists of precisely this failing:

> The jurists who believe in natural law seem to me to be in that naive state of mind that accepts what has been familiar and accepted by them and their neighbors as something that must be accepted by all men everywhere.[44]

The article avoided specific references; its argument remained general. But Holmes unmistakably implied a historical objection that natural law erred because it abstracted a realm of right from legal practices that had mundane social and historical origins.

By the analogy of law to prophesy, Holmes countered natural law with a functional definition of law. In talking of law as the reification of prophesy, he repeated, in more absolute and quasi-theological terms, his instrumental conception of law as the incidence of the exercise of state force—a definition that repeated passages from his judicial opinions.[45] At the same time the analogy suggested a grander image of lawyers and judges as prophets, participants in the communication of a transcendental message.

No doubt Holmes believed he had thoroughly rejected natural law. No doubt he thought he had critically exposed its wrongmindedness and destroyed its claims to acceptance as a serious or coherent theory of law. Yet there is room to doubt how thoroughly and consistently Holmes truly rejected the central tenets of natural law. First, there is the very fervor with which Holmes attacked natural law, even in his last article. Why, indeed, did he continue to assail the theory with such passion—and at a time when it was apparently sinking into oblivion? Long before Freud, Queen Gertrude in *Hamlet* was alerted by denial, observing "The lady doth protest too much, methinks." Second, Holmes's statement that he had rejected natural law in his youth is inaccurate. Third, there is the problem of the vision behind *Natural Law*—expressed, perhaps, in its style, too—that meaning derived from connection to a greater whole that was known to be, even if known to be unknowable in its details. Holmes

---

[43]*Id.* at 312.

[44]*Id.*

[45]*See* American Banana Co. v. United Fruit Co., 213 U.S. 347, 356 (1909) (opinion by Holmes, J.) (describing law as a "statement of the circumstances in which the public force will be brought to bear upon men through the courts").

expressed this vision in various essays and speeches.[46] In *Natural Law*, he wrote:

> It is enough for us that the universe has produced us and has within it, as less than it, all that we believe and love. If we think of our existence not as that of a little god outside, but as that of a ganglion within, we have the infinite behind us. It gives us our only but our adequate significance. A grain of sand has the same, but what competent person supposes that he understands a grain of sand? That is as much beyond our grasp as man. If our imagination is strong enough to accept the vision of ourselves as parts inseverable from the rest, and to extend our final interest beyond the boundary of our skins, it justifies the sacrifice even of our lives for ends outside of ourselves.[47]

This passage can be variously interpreted according to the mood of the reader. Likening man to a grain of sand or ganglion has been read as evidence of Holmes's gloom.[48] But the grain of sand also evoked an image of a beach, and Holmes used it to validate the meaning of the individual as part of a whole. So, too, the image of ganglion was meant, by emphasizing community and interaction, to validate the worth of the individual. He had previously used the image of a ganglion to connote the great man, the individual whose importance was not in question.[49]

---

[46]*E.g.*, *The Occasional Speeches of Justice Oliver Wendell Holmes* 162, 167 (M. Howe comp. 1962); O. Holmes, *Collected Legal Papers*, *supra* note 34, 166, 247–48, 270–71, 275.

Grey writes, "Holmes' infusion of the workaday world with intrinsic value, value conceived in aesthetic terms, was a remnant he always retained from his early Emersonian romanticism." Grey, *supra* note 15, at 857. But he minimizes the vision as a "remnant" and seeks to distinguish Holmes's views from Emerson's. *Id.* at 857–58. In contrast, White argues persuasively that the views Holmes expressed in his extrajudicial writings and speeches must be taken seriously, and he reminds us that it was just one such speech that led Roosevelt to take note of Holmes. White, *Holmes's "Life Plan": Confronting Ambition, Passion, and Powerlessness*, *supra* note 13, at 1475.

[47]*Natural Law*, in O. Holmes, *Collected Legal Papers*, *supra* note 34, at 316.

[48]*See* White, *The Integrity of Holmes' Jurisprudence*, *supra* note 16, at 634 (White cites to his previous reading that in turn cited to Howe's reading).

[49]*See John Marshall* (1901), in O. Holmes, *Collected Legal Papers, supra* note 34, at 267.

C. Personal Philosophy

Recognition of Holmes's continuity with transcendentalist and natural law tradition contributes to a more complete understanding of his life and his thought.[50] Holmes was a strong proponent of the philosophy of transcendentalism in college. He had been raised in the New England circle of transcendentalists that included Emerson and of which his father was a leading figure. His writings at college revealed assimilation of transcendentalist philosophy and exhibited personality traits that were to endure. Aichele observes, for instance, that his first college essay "displayed considerable disdain for those who preferred the life of events over that of ideas."[51] So, too, Holmes's later writings and speeches exalted the life of the intellect.[52] Political commitment to the abolitionist cause[53] also manifested his acceptance of transcendental values and natural rights.

Notwithstanding his forceful criticism of natural law, Holmes retained interest throughout his life in the champion of transcendentalism. In 1912 Sheehan remarked in passing in a letter that Holmes "had no sympathy with Emerson."[54] Holmes replied:

> You put it much too strongly when you say that I had no sympathy with Emerson. When he was breaking and I was still young, I saw him on the other side of the street and ran over and said to him: "If I

---

[50]Recent biographies have been criticized for failing to integrate the study of Holmes's personality and his thought, his life and his judging. *See* Boyer, *The Justice as Janus-Figure*, 2 *Yale J.L. and the Humanities* 417, 426 (1990), Lerner, *The Spirit and the Laws*, *The New Republic* 34, 36 (April 2, 1990); White, *Holmes's "Life Plan": Confronting Ambition, Passion, and Powerlessness*, *supra* note 13, at 1410; Note, *supra* note 18, 800, 804–05.

[51]G. Aichele, *Oliver Wendell Holmes, Jr., supra* note 3, at 27.

[52]He wrote of Montesquieu that "[l]ike Descartes or Kant, he commanded the future from his study more than Napoleon from his throne." *Montesquieu* (1900), in O. Holmes, *Collected Legal Papers*, *supra* note 34, at 264. In a speech he observed, "Until lately the best thing that I was able to think of in favor of civilization, apart from blind acceptance of the order of the universe, was that it made possible the artist, the poet, the philosopher, and the man of science." Speech (March 7, 1900), in *id.* at 248.

[53]His abolitionist politics may have stemmed from his mother rather than his father. The sources are not clear. *See generally* L. Baker, *supra* note 2, at 95.

[54]*Holmes-Sheehan Correspondence: The Letters of Justice Oliver Wendell Holmes and Canon Patrick Augustine Sheehan* 48 (D. Burton ed. 1976).

> ever do anything, I shall owe a great deal of it to you," which was true. He was one of those who set one on fire.[55]

In 1930, long after he supposedly rejected his early transcendentalism and embraced an instrumental philosophy of law, Holmes wrote in a letter that "[t]he only firebrand of my youth that burns to me as brightly as ever is Emerson."[56] Baker has identified passages in Holmes's later speeches that evoke specific passages from Emerson's writings.[57]

Furthermore, the mature Holmes's enthusiasm for Emerson is not an isolated aberration. His enthusiasm, of course, might be discounted as fondness for the writings of the family friend whom he had admired in his youth. But Holmes's reading list indicates that the contemporary philosopher whom he read most as an adult was the idealist Santayana. The work that he reread most often was Spinoza's *Ethics*, one of the most extreme formulations of idealist metaphysics in the seventeenth century. Between 1867 and 1929 Holmes read the *Ethics* at least five times, and he read various other works by and about Spinoza.[58] His letters repeatedly—more than a half dozen times to several different correspondents—expressed his basic sympathy with the writings of Santayana and Spinoza. Holmes explained that it was precisely Spinoza's view of the world with which he agreed and not Spinoza's effort to impose rigorous logical consistency on philosophy through use of geometric method. Holmes wrote in 1929, "It is [Spinoza's] view of the universe that is the thing. He sees it as I see it more nearly than any of the old that I can think of."[59]

---

[55]*Id.* at 51. Holmes went on in the letter to write that he did not consider Emerson as a thinker but rather as a poet "whose function is not to discern but to make us realize truth." *Id.*

[56]2 *Holmes-Pollock Letters: The Correspondence of Mr. Justice Holmes and Sir Frederick Pollock 1874–1932* 264 (M. Howe ed. 1942). He similarly praised Emerson's essay on Montaigne in 1923. *The Holmes-Einstein Letters: Correspondence of Mr. Justice Holmes and Lewis Einstein 1903–1935* 214 (J. Peabody ed. 1964). *See also id.* at 290 (quoting Emerson verse).

[57]*See* L. Baker, *supra* note 2, at 85–86.

[58]*See* entries in the so-called Black Book, Oliver Wendell Holmes, Jr., Papers, Harvard Law School Library, at 108 col. 2, 109 col. 2, 121 col. 2, and 131 col. 1; Little, *The Early Reading of Justice Oliver Wendell Holmes*, 8 *Harvard Library J.* 63, 175 (1954).

[59]2 *Holmes-Laski Letters*, *supra* note 37, at 1133. Holmes's enthusiasm for Dewey, which he expressed in almost identical language, may shed light on just what Holmes believed he found in and accepted from Dewey—but it would not necessarily support an interpretation of Holmes as a pragmatist. *See generally* Grey, *supra* note 15, at 869–70 (discussing evidence of Holmes's admiration for Dewey).

The survival of transcendentalist philosophical influences in Holmes's extrajudicial writings and speeches is compatible with the theory that Holmes divided his life—and his ideas—into different compartments. It is possible to understand his philosophical musings as recreational expressions of passion that he had learned to exclude from his legal work.[60]

There is little doubt that Holmes worked to compartmentalize his mental world, and the explicit, almost nostalgic, retention of idealist sympathies in his extrajudicial writings evinced the greater freedom that he permitted himself outside of his work world.[61] Of course, the presence of transcendentalist influence in his extrajudicial writings does not in any way reduce the historical or biographical importance of the continuity. The extrajudicial writings may well constitute Holmes's most important literary and intellectual legacy. Such writings exerted a powerful impact in their day.

D. Judicial Philosophy

It is questionable, however, how far Holmes succeeded in keeping the personal philosophy that he expressed in letters and speeches from surfacing in his legal work. The investigation of his relation to natural law confirms the compartmentalization of his life, but it also helps to reintegrate his philosophy and his judging. Holmes's theory of law affected his decisionmaking in important cases, and through the influence of his jurisprudential theory he exerted tremendous influence on legal developments after his death.[62]

---

[60]*See generally* White, *Holmes's "Life Plan": Confronting Ambition, Passion, and Powerlessness*, *supra* note 13, at 1474–79.

[61]*See generally* White, *Holmes as Correspondent*, *supra* note 13, at 1707, 1749–50, 1757.

[62]The constitutional positions that Holmes advocated in some dissenting opinions were ultimately vindicated. He also shaped the allocation of power between federal and state judiciary through the so-called Erie doctrine that was adopted after his death. Erie Railroad Co. v. Tompkins, 304 U.S. 64 (1937). The Erie doctrine requires federal courts to apply substantive law derived from state case law in certain cases, and it was supported by two separate arguments. First, it was argued that a federal statute meant to incorporate state case law as the rule of decision in such cases. Second, it was argued that the federal judiciary lacked authority to establish autonomous rules of decision in such cases. The second argument (lack of federal judicial power to promulgate common law rules) was supported by constitutional and philosophical considerations.

The Erie doctrine's repudiation of "general common law" by federal courts was an application of Holmes's rejection of natural law and of his view that

Holmes challenged natural law concepts in his judicial writings with remarkable consistency and passion. Despite the fervor that he brought to his opposition to natural law, he remained curiously indifferent to its practical legal consequences.[63] There is no reason to believe that his hostility to natural law stemmed from any legal doctrinal or institutional consequence that he associated with the natural law. On the contrary, his mature philosophical convictions preceded his work in specific areas of law, and the passion he brought to criticism of legal theory originated outside of any concern with specific rules or cases. Only as he became more familiar with legal practices did he learn to detect the operation of natural law ideas, and then he applied his philosophical criticism to them.[64]

He did not reject natural law reasoning in his judicial work because he associated it with undesirable legal consequences. His first significant legal article in 1870[65] set forth a functional theory of law but defended judicial lawmaking and protested codification by using arguments that natural law writers had advanced a generation before.[66] As he acquired experience as a judge, Holmes became sensitive to the loose fit between legal theory and its application in cases. Holmes would hardly have subscribed to the more recent notion

---

law was nothing other than what courts actually do. Formulations of the Erie doctrine were found in Holmes's prior dissents, and *Erie* itself relied on his arguments for authority on the nonexistence of a "transcendental body of law outside of any particular State." *Erie*, 304 U.S. at 78 (1937) (*quoting* Black & White Taxicab & Transfer Co. v. Brown & Yellow Taxicab & Transfer Co., 276 U.S. 518, 533 (1928) (Holmes, J., dissenting)).

The vindication of Holmes's views by the Erie doctrine was also symbolic, for the case overruled Swift v. Tyson, 41 U.S. (16 Pet.) 1 (1842), which Holmes had characterized as resting on a "fallacy and illusion." The "fallacy and illusion" were the natural law reasoning of *Swift*'s author, Justice Story.

[63]The Erie doctrine was proposed, championed, and adopted by federal judges who were motivated largely by abstract theories of law and the federal-state relationship. It is hard to see how state interests were frustrated before its adoption, for states had been able to require federal application of state rules of decision by enacting such state rules as positive law. It is possible that states benefitted from any forum shopping that the federal law encouraged before *Erie*.

[64]For example, Holmes raised no criticism of the practice of federal common lawmaking in 1872. *See* 1 J. Kent, *Commentaries on American Law* * 342 at 379–80 n.1 (12th ed. O. Holmes ed. 1873)(describing the practice without objection). But he elsewhere proposed an instrumental criticism of transcendental notions of law. *Id.* * 2 at 2 n.1.

[65]*Codes, and the Arrangement of the Law*, 5 *Am. L. Rev.* 1 (1870), reprinted in O. Holmes, *The Formative Essays*, *supra* note 16, at 77.

[66]*See* Story, *Codification of the Common Law*, in J. Story, *supra* note 28, at 698–734.

that law is nondeterminate; he insisted in *The Common Law* that law required articulable standards. Natural law judging did not offend him because of its results but rather because of its philosophical postulates.

The problematic impact of natural law on Holmes's judicial work might be explored in an exhaustive study of his opinions, but it is illustrated adequately by one case. In 1891, after Holmes had spent nine years on the Massachusetts bench, an appeal was taken to the Supreme Court from an opinion that Holmes had authored in the case of *Heard v. Sturgis*.[67] Holmes supported his decision in part by theoretical considerations that revealed his hostility to natural law. In reversing, the Supreme Court expressly invoked natural law arguments.

Holmes recorded his reaction to being reversed in a letter to his friend Pollock: "I think it [is] an interesting case and one which I could have written the other way, but I confess [that] I think the ground adopted by the U.S. Court one which is quite irreconcilable with primary juridical notions."[68] This reaction not only revealed an indifference to the result in the case; it showed, in a case with which he was intimately familiar, that he explicitly recognized that alternative results were compatible with his legal philosophy. What he protested with some emotion was precisely the philosophical justification, resting on natural law notions, that the Court advanced.

The dispute that was finally resolved in 1891 stemmed from events that took place almost thirty years earlier during the Civil War. The facts were not in dispute.[69] During the Civil War the plaintiffs had operated a shipping firm. Their shipping business had prospered, and they were solvent when they disbanded the business at the end of the war. During the next ten years, however, the plaintiffs encountered financial problems. In 1875 they were adjudicated bankrupt, and they made assignments in bankruptcy to the defendants.

---

[67]Heard v Sturgis, 146 Mass. 545 (1888), *reversed sub nom.* Williams v. Heard, 140 U.S. 529 (1891). C.A. Williams had represented the defendants unsuccessfully before the Massachusetts court, 146 Mass. at 546. C.A. William and Moses William represented the assignee on appeal, 140 U.S. at 529, but Moses William took an assignment of the defendant's interest and was substituted as party appellant before the Supreme Court, 140 U.S. at 529, 534.

Holmes wrote over one thousand opinions for the Massachusetts court. This was the only one that was reversed. *See* L. Baker, *supra*, note 2, at 274 n.*.

[68]1 *Holmes-Pollock Letters*, *supra* note 56, at 39–40.

[69]The case was submitted to the Supreme Judicial Court of Massachusetts upon an agreed statement of facts. 146 Mass. at 545.

The dispute concerned legal rights created by a fund established after the war. Great Britain had provided safe harbor to the enemy during the war, and United States claims against Britain were settled after the war by arbitration and treaty under which Great Britain made a payment to the United States for losses resulting from Confederate vessels sailing from British ports. The federal government administered disbursement of the funds to claimants. By 1882 claims for direct injury had been paid, so Congress provided for payments to persons who had paid extra premiums for war risk insurance during the Civil War. The plaintiffs' wartime shipping business had made such extra insurance premiums.

The legislation that provided for payments to persons who had paid war risk insurance premiums occurred many years after the plaintiffs' business had failed and after they had made assignments in bankruptcy. In 1886 a Court of Commissioners awarded the defendants the funds; the award discharged the government's obligation to pay but did not resolve the dispute between the plaintiffs and the defendants to the award. Consequently, the plaintiffs brought an action in Massachusetts state court against the defendants. The question for decision was whether the plaintiffs, who had paid the increased war risk insurance premiums, or the defendants, to whom the plaintiffs had assigned their assets during bankruptcy, were entitled to the funds.

The case compelled little sympathy for either party's cause, for the funds represented a windfall. Congress could have done anything with the money, and it had contemplated several alternatives, including absorbing the monies into the general treasury.[70] Without the legislation no one had a compelling legal or moral claim against the government. Furthermore, the problem for decision arose only because Congress had failed to resolve the issue of the respective priority of claims in the legislation.[71]

Holmes found for the plaintiffs in a carefully reasoned opinion. He argued that the plaintiffs had no claim of right against the government at the time of the assignment of their interests to the defendants; accordingly, he concluded that their claim to the fund was

---

[70]146 Mass. at 551. Holmes used the fact that Congress considered doing other things with the funds to buttress his construction of the legislation as establishing a gratuity rather than an entitlement. As he put it, Congress "hesitated long between several competing applicants." 146 Mass. at 551. Of course, his characterization was tendentious, for deliberation might equally have been construed as evincing a careful legislative deliberation of policy that imposed priorities on disbursement.

[71]The original legislation disbursing funds to persons who had suffered actual loss during the war mentioned assignees of claimants. 146 Mass. at 551.

a gratuity and did not pass to the defendants. The legal fictions and precedents that Holmes employed lent a curious twist to the form of his argument: the plaintiffs prevailed because of the weakness and unenforceability of their original claim to the government fund. This unstated major premise was shared by Holmes and by the Supreme Court, which reversed. Their differences touched on the proper characterization of the plaintiffs' interest, not in the legal consequences that resulted from the characterization.

The room for Holmes to maneuver was narrow once he accepted the major premise. It was settled law that when the government collected a fund on behalf of injured citizens from a foreign power, the claims of the citizens to the fund were treated *as if* they were rights that the government had a duty to recognize. It was also settled law that in such a case that the right-like claims to the funds would pass retroactively to an assignee, even where the assignment predated the establishment of the fund.[72]

Holmes recognized that he was bound by the decisions "as far as they go."[73] Although the prior decisions were supported by broad rhetorical opinions that articulated moral considerations as the grounds of decision, Holmes construed the decisions narrowly. His limitation of the precedent was clearly motivated by his hostility to the creation of legal rights from claims of moral obligations, and he turned to an abstract, theoretical discussion of the nature of sovereignty in order to expose the fictitious, counterfactual character of moral "rights" that were asserted against government:

> But it must be remembered, whenever a new statute comes up for consideration, that although it may be found by construction to give what it gives as if in pursuance of a legal duty, there is no such legal duty in fact, and no antecedent right on the part of the persons who receive its benefits. It is only tautologous to say that the law knows nothing of moral rights unless they are also legal right, and from before the days of Hobbes the argument has been public property

---

[72]Justice Story had held in a Supreme Court decision that such quasi-rights were assets that would be construed to pass retroactively to an assignee. Holmes referred to the case, 146 Mass. at 547, 548, and the Supreme Court relied on it and quoted language from it in reversing: "It is not universally, though it may ordinarily be one test of right, that it may be enforced in a court of justice. . . . Neither . . . Great Britain nor the government of the United States is suable in the ordinary courts of justice, for debts due by either; yet who will doubt that such debts are rights?" Comegys v. Vasse, 26 U.S. (1 Pet. 193, 216) 108, 118 (1828) (Story, J.) (quoted in Williams v. Heard, 140 U.S. at 555.) (I have omitted part of the text quoted by Lamar [ellipses added] and emended the punctuation slightly to correspond with the original.)

[73]146 Mass. at 548.

> that there is no such thing as a right created by law, as against the sovereign who makes the law by which the right is to be created.[74]

Citations to Hobbes, Bodin, Bentham, and Austin were added.

Holmes's hostility to transferrable claims of right against the government did leave two ways in which such a transferrable right could arise. First, such a right could have been established by legislation. Holmes, however, construed the statute to intend the payment as a gratuity.[75] Second, he felt constrained to read the cases as recognizing a transferrable right against the government when supported by a preexisting obligation. But he narrowly distinguished the kinds of claims that had been recognized in previous cases from the kind of claim that the plaintiffs asserted. Previous cases, Holmes insisted, had treated claims for distinct war-related losses and injuries that the government undertook to compensate.

Holmes reasoned that the increased cost of war risk insurance was not the kind of loss that supported an obligation:

> Inasmuch as presumably the cost of the war premiums in general ultimately fell upon the purchasers of insured goods, a claim against the government for indemnity in respect of them would resolve itself finally into a claim of all the members of the community for increased cost of living on account of the war.[76]

By distinguishing the previous cases, Holmes rejected them as authority that the plaintiffs' claim was a right that was transferred by the assignment in bankruptcy. Nevertheless, his argument implicitly accepted the major premise (which the cases arguably did not require) that a gratuity was not transferred by an assignment in

---

[74]146 Mass. at 549.

[75]The language was not clear, and Holmes read the other evidence of legislative history as "at least as favorable to the view that this payment of war premiums was by way of gratuity." 146 Mass. at 551.

[76]146 Mass. at 550. The reasoning supporting Holmes's rejection of increased insurance costs as a loss supporting an obligation repeated an argument that he had elaborated in *The Common Law* 96 (1881).

Application of economic analysis to the characterization of moral obligations in the *Heard* opinion illuminates the passage in *The Common Law*, which has usually been interpreted as an attempt to derive legal duty from economic considerations. But the work actually directed a moral argument against strict liability that was distinct from the argument directed against its economic inefficiency: "The undertaking to redistribute losses simply on the ground that they resulted from the defendant's act would not only be open to these [economic] objections, but, as it is hoped the preceding discussion has shown, *to the still graver one of offending the sense of justice.*" *Id.* at 96 (emphasis added).

bankruptcy. Notwithstanding the exposition of his views of sovereignty, the result actually flowed from his manipulation of ideas of imperfect obligation, which derived from natural law theory.

His judgment was paradoxical. In the end, he directed use of state force to compel the defendants to pay the proceeds of the government award to the plaintiffs for the reason that the plaintiffs had no claim of right to the funds against the government, from whom the defendants had acquired possession.

In the letter to Pollock, Holmes acknowledged that the legal issue—whether the plaintiffs' assignment in bankruptcy conveyed an interest that was created only after the assignment—could have been decided in various ways. His opinion made clear that the act of 1882 could have been construed so as to give the assignee the claim.[77] So, why did Holmes decide as he did? His opinion cannot be satisfactorily explained as arbitrary policy choice, for Holmes, ironically, cared far too little either way to make a choice on policy grounds.[78] Nor did the opinion express any real preference for deferring to the legislature.

The opinion did, however, express real emotion in its rejection of the natural law premises that derived a claim from an imperfect obligation. And Holmes again reacted with emotion to the appearance of those grounds in the reversal of his decision. In short, Holmes's decision seems to have been motivated by his desire to vanquish the natural law reasoning advanced by the defendant and adopted by two dissenting justices.

The Supreme Court reversed unanimously for the same reasons two justices had dissented from Holmes's decision. Conceding that Congress could have done anything with the money and that without the legislation neither plaintiffs nor their assignees had enforceable claims of right against either the United States government or Great Britain, the Court rejected Holmes's view that it thus followed that payments under the 1882 legislation were purely gratuitous. The Court found, on the contrary, that there was a preexisting moral obligation: "While . . . there were no means of compelling Congress to distribute the fund . . . and while the claimant was remediless . . ., nevertheless there was at all times a moral obligation on the part of the government to do justice to those who had suffered in property."[79] This imperfect obligation supported the existence of a right that

[77]He may also have considered application of defenses of equitable estoppel or waiver as ways to defeat the plaintiffs' action.

[78]White concludes from a study of Holmes's state court tort opinions that Holmes came to accept that "cases inevitably presented conflicts between desirable social principles, and judges simply had to choose." White, *The Integrity of Holmes' Jurisprudence*, *supra* note 16, at 649.

[79]140 U.S. at 540–41.

passed with property to the assignee in bankruptcy, even though the right only became enforceable after the assignment.

In reversing, the Court discussed the operation of the bankruptcy statute, which Holmes had ignored.[80] The Court also reasoned that the plaintiffs' right was an assignable interest because it had characteristic features of property. For example, the Court observed that the claim would have survived and been included as an asset of the estate in the event of the claimant's death.[81]

The Supreme Court's reasoning, especially its reliance on the idea of moral obligations to support legal rights, exemplified the older natural law approach to legal theory. By 1891 Holmes had been attacking natural law theory for years, and it was undoubtedly the natural law grounds of Justice Lamar's holding that so irritated him and that he complained were "irreconcilable with primary juridical notions."

It could be argued that Holmes's passionate objections to natural law blinded him to important countervailing considerations and contributed to a weak opinion. Preoccupied with the abstract problem of legal interests under the language of the 1882 legislation, Holmes ignored the policy goals of the bankruptcy statute that authorized the assignment to defendants. His hostility to natural law prevented him from even acknowledging its possible relevance as a guide to construction. For example, he did not entertain the possibility that natural law assumptions, if widely shared by Congress, might be relevant to construing legislative intent.

His hostility to natural law led him to distinguish precedent so narrowly that the distinction was not only unacceptable but apparently even incomprehensible to the two dissenting justices and to the unanimous Supreme Court, for in reversing, the Supreme Court supported its decision partly by reference to principles of natural justice. But the Court also clearly felt constrained by

---

[80]Justice Lamar wrote:

> [The bankruptcy act] puts the assigneee in the same position as regards all manner and description of the bankrupt's property (except that specifically exempt), as the bankrupt himself would have occupied had no assignment been made. And subsequent sections establish in the assignee the right to sue for and recover all the bankrupt's "estate, debts and effect" in his own name . . . .
>
> It must be conceded that the language of the [act] is broad and comprehensive enough to embrace the whole property of the bankrupt. Was the claim in this case "property" in any sense of the term? We think it was.

140 U.S. at 540.

[81]140 U.S. at 540, 541.

principles announced in prior Supreme Court cases[82] and by persuasive authority from a number of other courts.[83]

Holmes's decision in the *Heard* case illustrates some of the problems that arise in the study of the relationship between his legal philosophy and his judging. The decision also summarizes problems that arise in interpreting Holmes's philosophy of law. His criticism of natural law and his attempt to substitute an instrumental idea of law are clear in the opinion. The sources of his antagonism for natural law are far less clear; the sources of hostility are not even loosely related to the issues in the case. Moreover, the consciously controversial posture that Holmes took in the case ironically obscured the fact that he shared important doctrines and ideas with the legal philosophy that he sought to destroy.

Holmes did not question the premise supplied by natural law decisions that a gratuitous award would not transfer. His decision was grounded on the proper classification of the plaintiffs' claim. In classifying the claim as a gratuity, he employed natural law reasoning, arguing that it was not supported by a moral right or an imperfect obligation. To be sure, he proposed a new economic test for such an obligation, but the results of his test were compatible with the previous natural law cases.

Natural law and transcendentalist philosophy affected more than details of the structure of Holmes's argument in the *Heard* case. The opinion was marked by reasoning from absolutes and recourse to philosophical authority. He sought to distinguish and eliminate the effect of precedent that was inconsistent with his theory of sovereignty. Indifferent to the actual result, the case provided Holmes an occasion to combat his philosophical enemy and an opportunity to articulate more coherent and rational rules for judicial decision making. The opinion's theory of sovereignty, construction of legislation, and interpretation of precedent all manifested a search for freedom from authoritative rules; but the effort to free decision-making from external authority also revealed an extraordinary faith in the power of judges to reason and do justice.[84]

---

[82]146 Mass. at 558 (Field, J., dissenting)("I cannot distinguish the principles which should govern the case at bar from those declare in *Comegys v. Vasse*, and the other cases cited").

[83]146 Mass. at 556 (Field, J., dissenting) (discussing authority from the Court of Commissioners of Alabama Claims, Maine, New York, Maryland).

[84]Novick reduces Holmes's constitutional theory to an application to states of Cooley's theory of sovereignty. Under this view state legislative power replicated the self-defining power of Parliament. S. Novick, *supra* note 3, at 444 n.24.

This interpretation, however, is contradicted by Holmes's critical treatment of legislative power in scholarly writings, *e.g.*, *The Common Law, supra* note 76, at 96 (state interference is an "evil"), ***Montesquieu***, in O. Holmes, *Collected Legal Papers*, *supra* note 34, at 262 ("Montesquieu had a possibly exaggerated belief in the power of legislation"). More important, it is also contradicted by opinions in which Holmes applied constitutional law to exercises of legislative sovereignty. For example, in Fountleroy v. Lum, 210 U.S. 120 (1908), a Missouri judgment creditor sought to enforce the Missouri judgment in Mississippi state court. The judgment was based on an underlying contract that was criminal in Mississippi. Mississippi legislation provided that such contracts "shall not be enforced by any court." The Mississippi courts had followed the legislation and refused to enforce it.

In reversing, Holmes held that the statute did not deprive the Mississippi court of jurisdiction but "seems to us only to lay down a rule of decision." 210 U.S. at 235. The distinction between rule of decision and power to decide was, at least, an important rule of construction that decided the case. Such a distinction would have been meaningless if Holmes submitted to the supremacy of state legislation (subject only to federal constitutional limits), for the intent of the Mississippi legislature was not in doubt.

Indeed, it is arguable that Holmes's underlying views of judicial power directly affected the constitutional limits that he imposed on states. In a later case where state legislation deprived a state court of jurisdiction to enforce a foreign state judgment, Holmes did not hesitate to restore jurisdiction on constitutional grounds. *See* Kenney v. Supreme Lodge of the World, 252 U.S. 411 (1920).

CHAPTER 2

Philosophy at College

HOLMES entered Harvard in the fall of 1857 and graduated in the summer of 1861.[1] At college he published essays, reviews, and poetry in two student-edited periodicals, *The Harvard Magazine* and *The University Quarterly*. The pieces appeared anonymously, but Holmes's authorship was known to readers, and the writings have been discussed by his biographers.[2] He apparently considered his college work to be significant, for in 1873 he compiled four of the publications together with his *American Law Review* articles in a volume with a hand-written title page:

Essays
from
The Harvard Magazine
University Quarterly
and

---

[1]Treatments of Holmes's college experiences include L. Baker, *The Justice From Beacon Hill: The Life and Times of Oliver Wendell Holmes* 72–102 (1991); M. Howe, *Justice Oliver Wendell Holmes: The Shaping Years 1841–1870* 35–79 (1975); S. Bent, *Justice Oliver Wendell Holmes: A Biography* 56–72 (1932); G. Aichele, *Oliver Wendell Holmes, Jr.: Soldier, Scholar, Judge* 25–36 (1989); S. Novick, *Honorable Justice: The Life of Oliver Wendell Holmes* 20–28 (1989); *Introduction* to O. Holmes, *The Mind and Faith of Justice Holmes: His Speeches, Essays, Letters and Judicial Opinion* xxi–xxiii (M. Lerner ed. 1946); C. Bowen, *Yankee from Olympus* 105–33 (1944); Fiechter, *The Preparation of an American Aristocrat*, 6 *New Eng. Q.* 3, 4–5 (1933).

[2]In 1914 Holmes's classmate Frank Warren Hackett prepared an index of *The Harvard Magazine* from notes dating back to period of Hackett's and Holmes's work on the journal. The Hackett index is preserved in the Harvard University Archives and identifies Holmes as author of the articles. The publications are discussed in L. Baker, *supra* note 1, at 89–92, Fiechter, *supra* note 1, at 8–13, M. Howe *supra* note 1, at 43–62, Aichele, *supra* note 1, at 27–30, and Novick, *supra* note 1, at 27–28. The archives also hold an index to volumes one through ten of the *Magazine*, compiling the attribution of works from handwritten notes in copies of the *Magazine* that the Archives received.

American Law Review
By
O.W. Holmes Jr.
December 1858
July 1873

The volume included his three earliest essays: ***Books, Notes on Albert Durer*** [*sic*], ***Plato***, and his sophomore poem ***Alma Mater***.[3] In the mid 1880s Holmes had this volume professionally bound in a handsome leather and board binding. The leather spine bore the printed gilt title "Essays/O.W. Holmes Jr." The bound volume assembled publications through 1884, but Holmes continued to paste articles and manuscripts into blank pages at the end of the volume up to February 1891.

Despite recent interest in Holmes's intellectual biography,[4] and notwithstanding the growing scholarship on his early *American Law Review* articles,[5] the college writings have attracted little attention.[6] The college writings illuminate an important but little understood period in Holmes's intellectual development.

The writings seem largely indifferent to law. They were exercises in philosophy and criticism, heavily influenced by the transcendentalism of Emerson and by the aesthetic naturalism of

---

[3]Oliver Wendell Holmes, Jr., Papers, Harvard Law School Library, Manuscript Box 18. Note that Holmes in his essay on Dürer and in all of his references to the painter always spelled the artist's name as "Durer."

[4]*E.g.*, S. Novick, *supra* note 1; H. Pohlman, *Justice Oliver Wendell Holmes & Utilitarian Jurisprudence* (1984); O. Holmes, *Progressive Masks: Letters of Oliver Wendell Holmes, Jr., & Franklin Ford* (D. Burton ed. 1982); Grey, *Holmes & Legal Pragmatism*, 41 *Stan. L. Rev.* 787–870 (1989).

[5]*See* O. Holmes, *The Formative Essays of Justice Holmes: The Making of an American Legal Philosophy* 77–259 (F. Kellogg ed. 1984); LaPiana, *Victorian from Beacon Hill: Oliver Wendell Holmes's Early Legal Scholarship*, 90 *Colum. L. Rev.* 809 (1990).

[6]They are reprinted in Hoffheimer, *The Early Critical and Philosophical Writings of Justice Holmes*, 30 *B.C.L. Rev.* 1221, 1250–82 (1989). Holmes's marginal emendations suggest that he may have considered republishing the essays at one time. Howe's transcription of the early essays also suggests that he may have been preparing them for publication at one time. Copies of the originals that Holmes retained and of Howe's typescripts survive. The Oliver Wendell Holmes, Jr., Papers (University Publications of America, 1985) (Microfilm Project) reels 65 & 67. Charles Warren discussed the early writings in an unpublished essay entitled "Undergraduate Writings of Adams, Holmes, and Garrison." Charles Warren Papers, Harvard Law School Library. Only one essay was previously reprinted: Holmes, *Albert Durer*, appended to Stechow, *Justice Holmes' Notes on Albert Durer*, 8 *J. Aesthetics & Art Criticism* 119, 122–24 (1949).

Ruskin. Yet at the time the last college essays were published, Holmes wrote, "If I survive the war I expect to study law as my profession or at least for a starting point."[7]

The college works disclose the origins of fundamental interests and attitudes that Holmes retained throughout his life. His interest in philosophy, so evident in the college essays, continued during[8] and after[9] the war. In 1866 and 1867 Holmes was studying philosophy intensively and, in rereading his college essay on *Plato*, made marginal notes to his copy of the article in 1867. The early writings shed light on important changes in his philosophical views. While his early writings expressed commitment to the idealist philosophical principles of transcendentalism,[10] in later years Holmes criticized the views of his father's generation; he distinguished himself from the "scientific[]" upbringing of his father, and he referred to a great gulf that separated his views from his father's.[11]

Holmes looked back in later years with disappointment on the distinguished career of his accomplished father. Though his father was a leading figure in the transcendentalist movement, a respected physician, poet, novelist, and critic, Holmes came to believe that his father had produced nothing "great" and that his talented father had dissipated his efforts in cosmopolitan or dilettante works.[12] In later years Holmes repeatedly manifested his fear of dissipation: he cautioned aspiring lawyers against wasting their time in the study of Roman law, an esoteric subject not necessary for the mastery of contemporary legal practice;[13] he warned his young friend Wu against spending a year in the study of the work of the philosopher Spinoza,

---

[7]Holmes, *Autobiographical Sketch*, in Fiechter, *supra* note 1, at 5; O. Holmes, *The Mind & Faith of Justice Holmes*, *supra* note 1, at 8.

[8]*E.g.*, Holmes, fragment dated April 18, 1864, in O. Holmes *Touched with Fire: Civil War Letters and Diary* 95–97 (M. Howe ed. 1969).

[9]Holmes recorded his reading after the war. *See* Little, *The Early Reading of Justice Oliver Wendell Holmes*, 8 *Harv. Lib. Bull.* 163 (1954); *M. Howe*, *supra* note 1, at 255–56.

[10]*See, e.g.*, L. Fuller, *The Law in Search of Itself* 106–07 (1940); H. Pohlman, *supra* note 4, at 9; Grey, *supra* note 4, at 788; Howe, *The Positivism of Mr. Justice Holmes*, 64 *Harv. L. Rev.* 529 (1951); P. Wiener, *Evolution & the Founders of Pragmatism* (1969); F. Kellogg, *Preface* to O. Holmes, *The Formative Essays of Justice Holmes*, *supra* note 5, at xi–xii; Kelley, *Oliver Wendell Holmes, Utilitarian Jurisprudence, and the Positivism of John Stuart Mill*, 30 *Am. J. Juris.* 189 (1985).

[11]*See The Holmes-Cohen Correspondence*, 9 *J. Hist. Ideas* 3, 14–15 (1948).

[12]*See* Holmes's letter to Stevens, July 26, 1914, *quoted in part* in M. Howe, *supra* note 1, at 19.

[13]*See* O.W. Holmes, *The Bar as a Profession* (1896), in O. Holmes, *Collected Legal Papers* 153, 155–57 (1921).

though Holmes himself praised Spinoza's philosophy and read Spinoza repeatedly.[14]

Holmes's later work represented a reaction against his earlier attitudes, and his critical judgment of his father's dissipation may have also reflected his mature negative judgment of his own early efforts. He stopped adding to the volume that contained the college writings in 1891, and he did not include them in his *Collected Legal Papers* (1921).

Holmes's intensive legal studies after the Civil War resulted in a series of important legal publications, culminating in *The Common Law* (1881). His postwar writings eschewed the broad topical coverage and sweeping generalization of his early articles. In pursuing law, as announced at the end of college, Holmes abandoned aspirations to philosophy, letters, and poetry. The narrowing of his scholarship reflected his assimilation of insular traditions of English-language legal scholarship. It reflected also a shift in his attitude toward scholarship. He came to believe that important work was produced by the expert who concentrated effort on the narrow and technical problem. The break with his earlier views was not sudden, however, and Holmes himself demonstrated awareness of continuity. Long after he completed *The Common Law*, he continued to compile his revolutionary writings on legal theory together with the college publications.

Though excluding art and poetry from his scholarship, Holmes still retained broad literary and philosophical interests until his death; nevertheless, he relegated those interests to a sphere of personal life, as reflected in his readings, private correspondence, and conversation and other extrajudicial utterances.[15] He abandoned his academic study of the German painter and engraver Dürer, but at his death over seventy years later his private upstairs sitting room in Beverly Farms was decorated with six framed copies of works by Dürer.[16]

---

[14]Letter to Wu, July 26, 1923, O. Holmes, *Justice Holmes to Dr. Wu* (n.d. [1935]); O. Holmes, *Justice Oliver Wendell Holmes: His Uncollected Letters and Papers* 166 (H. Shriver ed. 1936). Novick treats Holmes's interest in Spinoza as merely escapist diversion. *See* S. Novick *supra* note 1, at 236, 313, 361. Other recent biographies ignore it altogether.

[15]Baker suggests that Holmes's specialization in legal scholarship reflected the influence of Shattuck and Holmes's experiences in legal practice. *See* L. Baker, *supra* note 1, at 194–95. White discusses the compartmentalization of Holmes's personality, as reflected in his writings. White, *Holmes as Correspondent*, 43 *Vand. L. Rev.* 1707 (1990).

[16]*See* the inventory of Holmes's estate, The Oliver Wendell Holmes, Jr., Papers, *supra* note 6, reel 17.

Holmes's early writings revealed original and critical efforts to apply transcendentalist philosophy and to confront inherent problems in that philosophy. Although his early efforts led to an intellectual impasse, he did not abandon the efforts and understood his later legal scholarship, even in its more mundane aspects, as pursing the philosophical inquiry that had begun at college.[17]

The early writings provide the starting point for serious study of Holmes and indeed illuminate a critical problem in American legal history. The problem of the relation between Holmes's early and later writings is representative of the broader problem of the relation between transcendentalism and positivism—natural law and formalism. As long as transcendentalism and formalism are considered to be incompatible and mutually exclusive, then Holmes's intellectual development can be explained only as a simple volte-face—and his college writings can be safely ignored as juvenilia. But the antithetical relation between transcendentalism and formalism is questionable,[18] and Holmes's intellectual biography illustrates the complex symbiotic relation between the two.

A. Ralph Waldo Emerson

Holmes's college essays followed an Emersonian model. The transcendentalist philosophical perspective and praise of Emerson's work obviously revealed the author's enthusiasm for Emerson. The Emersonian model was reflected also in the style of Holmes's articles—their homiletic tone, reliance on analogy, internal dialogue with other texts, frequent shifts of person and mood, repetitious use of passive voice or weak verbs, and use of pithy apothegms. Holmes's father aptly described Emerson's style as "epigrammatic, incisive, authoritative, sometimes quaint. . . . His paragraphs are full of brittle sentences that break and fall apart and are independent units, like the fragments of a coral colony. His imagery is frequently daring, leaping from the concrete to the abstract."[19] In Emerson and in Holmes's earliest work, quotations and references were mustered like illustrations and incorporated into the text for their effect on the ear rather than as authority or source. Voices from widely separated times and cultures were brought together with naive disregard of

---

[17]*See* Letter to Emerson in 1876, *quoted in* M. Howe, *O.W. Holmes, Jr.: Counselor-At-Law* 8 (1948); Letter to Pollock, March 5, 1881, in O. Holmes, *1 Holmes-Pollock Letters: The Correspondence of Mr. Justice Holmes and Sir Frederick Pollock 1874–1932* 16 (M. Howe ed. 1942).

[18]*E.g.*, Horowitz, *History and Theory*, 96 *Yale L.J.* 1825, 1835 (1987).

[19]O. Holmes, [Sr.,] *Emerson* 403–04 (1890).

their dissimilar contexts.[20] Holmes's readers would have appreciated the contextual resonance.

Changes in style in Holmes's early writings reflected important changes in his attitude toward transcendentalism. The earliest essay was most indebted to Emerson: *Books* was modeled closely on Emerson's article of the same title, which had appeared anonymously in the January 1858 issue of *The Atlantic Monthly*.[21] Emerson's article provided sources for statements that Holmes made throughout the essay. Holmes advised reading only those works that engaged the reader: "[I]t is best to read what we like." Emerson had advised:

> Never read any but what you like; or, in Shakspeare's [sic] phrase,
> —"No profit goes where is no pleasure ta'en:
> In brief, sir, study what you most affect."[22]

Holmes discussed the proliferation of published works and the impossibility of reading more than a few of them—"Books are now almost innumerable." Emerson had similarly written of the proliferation of published titles—"the number of extant printed books may . . . [exceed] a million."[23] Holmes proposed reading the classics, for "every grand book carries with it and implies ten thousand lesser

---

[20]Emerson's style reflected his method of composition. *See* 4 *The Collected Works of Ralph Waldo Emerson* 381 (W. Williams & D. Wilson eds. 1987). The method of composition, however, reflected his stylistic purposes.

[21]Emerson, *Books*, 1 *The Atlantic Monthly*, Jan. 1858, at 343–53. Though articles appeared anonymously, readers would have known the identity of important contributors. Because Holmes's essay referred to Emerson's article, it was probably composed after Emerson's had appeared in print. There is a possibility, however, that Holmes heard Emerson lecture from notes for the article and later added the citation to the published article.

I have been unable to fix the prepublication history of Emerson's 1858 essay. His diary refers simply to "Books" in late 1857. *See* 14 *The Journals and Miscellaneous Notebooks of Ralph Waldo Emerson* 457 (S. Smith & H. Hayford eds. 1978). Emerson later made minor changes to the essay and republished it as the eighth essay in the collection R. Emerson, *Society and Solitude* (1870), in 7 *Emerson's Complete Works* 187–221 (E. Emerson ed. 1904).

The topic of books had engaged Emerson repeatedly. He lectured more than once on the topic in the late 1840s. *See* G. Allen, *Waldo Emerson* 525 (1981). He lectured again on the topic December 25, 1864; an incomplete text and summary of the lecture was published at that time, which has been reprinted. *See* R. Emerson, *Society and Solitude* 39–42 (C. Gohdes ed. 1932).

[22]Emerson, *Books*, *supra* note 21, at 346; *see also* R. Emerson, *Society and Solitude*, supra note 21, at 196.

[23]Emerson, *Books*, *supra* note 21, at 345; *see also* R. Emerson, *Society and Solitude*, *supra* note 21, at 193.

ones," condensing two themes that he found in Emerson—the articulation of experience of a culture in that culture's great literary work and the beneficial selective process of history by which less important works were forgotten.[24] Holmes's praise of Herodotus's use of anecdotes echoed Emerson's praise.[25] Even the image with which Holmes concluded the essay—an image of books as dormant seeds that spring up—suggested passages where Emerson had written of books as "vital and spermatic," of Plato in which one finds "modern Europe in its causes and seed," of Robertson's history of Charles V, "a time of seeds and expansions, whereof our recent civilization is the fruit."[26]

Holmes differed with Emerson occasionally as to the valuation of some book or author. He disparaged Thomas a Kempis, for example, whom Emerson praised. Holmes and Emerson also differed significantly in tone. Emerson tended to view the proliferation of mediocre works with melancholy, while Holmes looked with optimism to a future literature of "Shakespeares and Prophets."[27] For the most part, however, Holmes appeared as advocate of Emerson's ideas. Holmes's originality in the essay lay in his condensation of Emerson's argument, the language in which he recast it, and the uses to which he put it.

---

[24]Emerson, *Books*, *supra* note 21, at 345–47; *see also* R. Emerson, *Society and Solitude*, *supra* note 21, at 195–201.

[25]"Herodotus, whose history contains inestimable anecdotes, which brought it with the learned into a sort of disesteem; but in these days, when it is found that what is most memorable of history is a few anecdotes, and that we need not be alarmed though we should find it not dull, it is regaining credit." Emerson, *Books*, *supra* note 21, at 346; R. Emerson, *Society and Solitude*, *supra* note 21, at 197–98. Emerson also had identified the importance of the Greek comic poets as a source for contemporary historians. Emerson, *Books*, *supra* note 21, at 347; R. Emerson, *Society and Solitude*, *supra* note 21, at 201–02. Holmes wrote:

> Little things—anecdotes—Will often display the whole manners and customs of a period, when we should have laid down the statistics as ignorant as we took them up. What is most pleasant about Herodotus is, that, in a history of the great nations of the earth, he tells us such facts as that the mares that gained three races are buried by the side of their master. . . . This history, which we can by no possibility get, except by fragments from contemporary plays and poems.

Holmes, *Books*.

[26]Emerson, *Books*, *supra* note 21, at 346, 349; R. Emerson, *Society and Solitude*, *supra* note 21, at 197–98, 206.

[27]*Compare with* Emerson, *Books*, *supra* note 21, at 345; R. Emerson, *Society and Solitude*, *supra* note 21, at 193–95.

Emerson's views were neither new nor unpopular by the late 1850s. Holmes had expressed special interest in Emerson during his first year at Harvard, and his parents gave him copies of Emerson's major works for his birthday, including both series of *Essays*, *English Traits*, *Representative Men* (which included the essay on Plato), and a volume of *Poems*.[28]

Defending Emerson, however, was a radical act for a Harvard student, because the faculty viewed transcendentalism with deep hostility, and Harvard's religious conservatives were scandalized by Emerson's theology. Emerson had not been invited back to Harvard for twenty years after delivering his address "The American Scholar," and in 1858 there was no indication that faculty attitudes were changing.

Holmes pressed Emerson into service against the college orthodoxy. Relating the topic of book reading to student life, Holmes imparted a combative edge to the argument that was not present in Emerson's article. Holmes scorned Calvinist theology: "A hundred years ago we burnt men's bodies for not agreeing with our religious tenets; we still burn their souls." He assailed fellow students who defended religious dogma unthinkingly and who failed to question slavery. He pointedly praised non-Christian religious scriptures, lambasting the ignorance of orthodox condemnations of such works and emphasizing the hypocritical failure of contemporary Christians to observe the Gospels' message of charity and forbearance.

Throughout his college writings Holmes voiced his views in deliberate opposition to the theological and academic orthodoxy, revealing the iconoclastic spirit that led him in college to join the liberal religious organization, the Christian Union. He explained at the end of college that he was motivated to join the Christian Union primarily by the desire to express opposition to the orthodox student group, the Christian Brethren.[29]

Holmes's seemingly unobjectionable humanist praise in *Plato* for the ethics of Socrates and Plato—"these two grand old heathen"—was a challenge to orthodox religious sensibilities. Plato was strongly identified with Emerson.[30] In *Notes on Albert Durer*, Holmes applied

---

[28]L. Baker, *supra* note 1, at 85. Holmes also received a volume of Emerson's lectures from Johnny Morse, and he had access at home to other works of Emerson. *Id.*

[29]Holmes, *Autobiographical Sketch*, in Fiechter, *supra* note 1, at 4–5; O. Holmes, *The Mind and Faith of Justice Holmes*, *supra* note 1; *see also* M. Howe, *supra* note 1, at 47–48, L. Baker, *supra* note 1, at 75–76.

[30]In the 1861 issue of *Harvard Magazine*, Hackett wrote humorously: "Plato, one of the most famous men of antiquity, is celebrated for . . . having been a warm friend and personal admirer of Mr. R. W. Emerson." *Quoted in* L. Baker, *supra* note 1, at 89.

to religion the historicism deriving from Emerson that he had previously applied to scholarship in *Books*. He associated the power of Dürer's pictorial representations with the artist's naive faith and wrote romantically of the days before the decline of faith. Such faith, Holmes suggested, remained vital in his day only for the ignorant and illiterate while the intelligent, moved by "noble philosophy," sought the future construction of an abstract religion. He associated enlightened religious views with the "growth of civilization" and contrasted modern abstract religion to the "paramount importance attached in darker times to the form of the story embodying the popular religion," which his readers would have understood as referring to contemporary conservative theology.

Holmes was only adopting familiar transcendentalist teaching in identifying the "ideal spirit" behind religion with humanist values shared by non-Christian cultures: he wrote that the ideal spirit "inspired the philosopher Plato . . . as well as the Christian Durer." Readers recognized the oblique partisan thrust of the abstract discussion, and one conservative student responded, protesting Holmes's idealization of abstract religion and contempt for traditional faith. The critic accused Holmes of mimicking Emerson and attacked Holmes's views as "barbarous in the province of reason and practical piety."[31] Soon after the appearance of the issue that contained Holmes's article on Dürer, the college president wrote to Holmes's father, threatening the suspension of the publication on the grounds of disrespectful words directed at a retiring faculty member.[32]

Holmes was hardly isolated in his stand against orthodoxy. Polarization of the student body mirrored the polarization of New England intellectuals. The intellectual battle was not fought in terms of a generational conflict for Holmes. Emerson was a family friend, Holmes's father's age. Holmes's father, himself a champion of transcendentalism and critic of the established orthodoxy on the faculty, not only gave Holmes Emerson's major writings; but he also wrote a spirited partisan article for the first issue of *The University Quarterly*.[33] The elder Holmes, when drawn into ongoing disciplinary skirmishes between Holmes and the college, most likely sympathized with his son.[34]

The younger Holmes had little sympathy or patience for much of the college curriculum. He absorbed ideas with enthusiasm from

---

[31]*See* M. Howe, *supra* note 1, at 59.

[32]The episode is discussed by L. Baker, *supra* note 1, at 88–89; M. Howe, *supra* note 1, at 59–60, 62.

[33]1 *University Quarterly* at 21, *quoted in part in* M. Howe *supra* note 1, at 60.

[34]*See* L. Baker, *supra* note 1, at 88–89, 99; M. Howe *supra* note 1, at 60, 69–70, 75, 77–78.

extracurricular sources like Emerson; but if he associated transcendentalist philosophy with progress, he did not particularly associate it with younger thinkers. On the contrary, he relied on the older generation of transcendentalists for authority in his college articles. He wrote with the voice of that generation. The pedagogic tone of *Books* separated the writer from his college reader and identified the author with the older generation; it was the voice of age and experience in *Books* that referred to "College gossip," to "students who while still young," and to "boyish insipidity." Whether passing judgment positively—as on Emerson—or more negatively —as on Ruskin—Holmes wrote with authority that verged on presumption and that disclosed unflinching confidence in the power of his own opinion: in *Notes on Albert Durer*, for example, he proposed to discuss a Raphael painting of which he had seen only an engraved copy!

The pervasive identification with views of his father's generation conflicted radically with the gulf that Holmes later believed existed between his ideas and his father's. Nevertheless, the college essays themselves contain indications of important views and sources that anticipate Holmes's later, more critical attitude toward transcendentalism. Holmes's continuing exoteric commitment to transcendentalism appeared throughout the college writings. He championed transcendentalist doctrine in part because it was established as emblem in the battle against orthodox narrowmindedness. But the visible advocacy of transcendentalism concealed internal changes in his attitudes toward transcendentalist doctrine. His later college writings evidenced the influence of sources and the adoption of key ideas that were inconsistent with transcendentalism; yet the internal intellectual discord led Holmes to embrace transcendentalism with renewed fervor and to seek to elaborate a broader philosophical scheme that would validate and reinforce transcendentalist insights.

B. Plato and Science

Holmes's article *Plato* represented a sustained philosophical inquiry. Handwritten notes on Holmes's copy of the article and the article's explicit references give some indication of the breadth of his study. It included translations from or references or citation to: *Theaetetus*, *Letters*, *Gorgias*, *Phaedrus*, *Timaeus*, *Phaedo*, and *Republic*. It cited and referred to two contemporary English philosophers, George Henry Lewes and William Whewell. Handwritten annotations referred to a translation of Heinrich Ritter's study of Plato.

Platonic philosophy and Plato's person had an electrified meaning for Holmes. He had been brought up in awe of Socrates and Plato, and they had been part of his early childhood education.[35] He approached Plato, as he later wrote Learned Hand, "expecting to find the secrets of life revealed."[36] In 1860 Holmes translated and delivered part of the *Apology* during exercises at Harvard. An anonymous notation on a program of the performances recorded that Holmes's delivery was "good."[37]

In the writings of Emerson he found Plato idolized.[38] Emerson's view of Plato was not naive, and Emerson's writings contained suggestions that Holmes developed critically in his article. Emerson acknowledged that Plato had no system and failed to make the transition from ideas to matter; he concluded that Plato was internally inconsistent, that "admirable texts can be quoted on both sides of every great question from him."[39] Yet Emerson embraced the contradictions and defended the value of Plato against critics by arguing that the critics misunderstood the aims of Plato and thus unfairly accused Plato of failing to achieve results he did not attempt.

---

[35]A childhood composition book, titled "O.W. Holmes, Oct. 13th 1848," has two entries on "Socrates the Philosopher," dated February 15, 1850, and one on "Plato," dated March 8, 1850. Oliver Wendell Holmes, Jr. Papers, *supra* note 6. But the contents of this composition book do not necessarily indicate his childhood interests or thoughts. The entries may have been transcriptions of the teacher's recitations. *But see* L. Baker, *supra* note 1, at 69 (taking the seven-year-old Holmes's statement that "there are a great many things better than gold" as evidence of an early antimaterialist spirit). Even if the contents were not original, they demonstrate the kinds of ideas to which Holmes was exposed at an early age.

[36]Letter to Learned Hand, May 6, 1924, *quoted in* M. Howe, *supra* note 1, at 34.

[37]Holmes, *Selection from the Apology of Socrates*, in *Commencement Performance 1859–60* item 33, Harvard University Archives. The note on the program is in Oliver Wendell Holmes, Jr., Papers, Harvard Law School Library, Manuscript Box 69. Holmes's interest in Greek was reflected in the submission that won the prize for best Greek composition. *See* 7 *Harvard Magazine* July 1861, at 362. The manuscript (translated as Appendix B in this volume) is in the Harvard University Archives.

[38]Emerson's notebooks contained so many references to Plato that Emerson himself compiled an "Index Platonia" to the references. *See* 4 *The Collected Works of Ralph Waldo Emerson*, *supra* note 20, at 382. Holmes's father actually ventured once to count various authors to whom Emerson referred in his published works. If we combine references to Plato and Socrates, they total 125. The next most frequently cited author was Shakespeare, with 112. O. Holmes [Sr.,], *supra* note 19, at 382.

[39]R. Emerson, *Representative Men, in 4 The Collected Works of Ralph Waldo Emerson, supra* note 20, at 43.

Emerson also accused critics of having unfairly blamed Plato for failing to accomplish what no philosophy had ever achieved—the explanation of existence.[40] Emerson responded to Plato's detractors with a marvelous image, comparing Plato with the great monuments of art, "like Karnac."

In Emerson, Holmes also found a progressive historical appreciation of Plato. For Emerson, Plato's thought summarized a past epoch,[41] and his thought retained vitality because of its genetic relation to the succeeding ages and to the present. The value of Plato's thought for Emerson derived not from its science or results but from its questioning spirit and confidence in the power of thought itself.

In criticizing Plato's lack of system and internal inconsistencies, Holmes elaborated longstanding criticisms that Emerson had acknowledged but deprecated. In valuing the dialectical inquiry and the artistic vision of Plato, Holmes followed Emerson. Holmes did not offer an original, critical reading of Plato in the essay, and he was no doubt disappointed by Emerson's reaction to the essay: "I have read your piece. When you strike at a king, you must *kill* him."[42] Emerson's dismissal of the essay probably reflected his conclusion that Holmes's had failed to advance beyond views that Emerson had previously criticized.

The lack of internal references to Emerson in *Plato*, unlike *Books*, reflected Holmes's greater assimilation of the transcendentalist philosophy. At the same time, the essay expressed critical differences with Emerson, especially in its treatment of historical progress. Holmes's devaluation of the emblem that Emerson's text had raised for Plato exemplified the divergence. Where Emerson had marveled at the ruins of ancient Near Eastern monuments, Holmes protested in a footnote that "these very structures . . . owed their magnificence to a semi-barbarian disregard of the life of the lower classes by those in power." While avoiding reference to Emerson, *Plato* explicitly cited recent works by Lewes and Whewell, English philosophers whose works set forth schematically and chronologically the history of philosophical ideas. Both Lewes and Whewell adopted a progressive and evolutionary theory of philosophical knowledge; both treated the history of ideas internally; both characterized the development of philosophy as alternating between idealist and empirical or

---

[40]*Id.*

[41]*Id.* at 44.

[42]*Quoted in* E. Sergeant, *Fire Under the Andes* 315 (1927); *see also* Holmes's letters to Sergeant, July 15 and December 7, 1926, in The Oliver Wendell Holmes, Jr. Papers, *supra* note 6, reel 37. *See generally* L. Baker, *supra* note 1, at 90–91.

sensationalist theories of knowledge. Lewes culminated his history with an enthusiastic treatment of Comte[43] whereas Whewell criticized Comte's attempt to reduce causal explanation to descriptive laws.[44]

The tone and organization of *Plato* comported with the kinds of treatments of individual philosophers that Holmes read in the histories of Lewes and Whewell. First, Holmes defined the goals of Socrates and Plato; next, he attempted objectively to describe chief features of their philosophy, illustrating with quotation and paraphrase; then he discussed internal weaknesses and inconsistencies; finally, he evaluated positive, enduring features and related Plato to modern views. Behind the sequential treatment was an implicit dichotomy of philosophy into idealist or empiricist theories, reflecting the cataloguing treatment of philosophic explanations by both Lewes and Whewell.

Holmes criticized Plato for failing to elaborate an adequate system of philosophy and related this to the inability of Plato's epistemology to differentiate different types of ideas:

> [T]here is a serious confusion introduced into the system, owing to the admitting equally, without distinction, the simple ideas like those on which mathematical truth is dependent, or perhaps, like beauty, which alone are recognized by our intuitive faculty . . . and the *complex* conceptions of table and chair, which are evidently mere arbitrary combinations effected by man; or still further, those like *humanity*, which is a purely general statement, drawn from observation, of a present fact.

The distinction between complex and simple ideas, current since Descartes, represented no challenge to an idealist theory of knowledge. But the dichotomy between necessary and contingent truths, and the relation of the latter to observation, reflected Holmes's interest in the empirical origin of factual knowledge and his movement away from transcendentalism.[45] Because of Holmes's continuing preoccupation with art, the divergence from

---

[43]*See* 4 G. Lewes, *A Biographical History of Philosophy* 245–64 (1852). Lewes also expounded Comte's philosophy in G. Lewes, *Comte's Philosophy of the Sciences* (1853). Someone in the Holmes family withdrew this volume from the Athenaeum in 1859 and 1860. *See* M. Howe, *supra* note 1, 53.

[44]*E.g.*, W. Whewell, *On the Philosophy of Discovery* 228–29 (1971) (reprint of 1860 ed.). Another work that Holmes cited in *Plato* sharply criticized Comte. *See* J. Devey, *Logic: Or the Science of Inference* 289–90, 293 (1864).

[45]Contrast Emerson's treatment of experience in R. Emerson, *Essays: Second Series*, essay 2 (1844).

transcendentalism remained undeveloped, and the internal tension remained subdued. Art remained within the realm of objects proper to idealist epistemology, and, while viewing negatively Plato's failure to elaborate a coherent system of philosophy, Holmes praised Plato's separation of ideal and real man as anticipating the best art.[46]

There was a close fit between transcendentalist doctrine and its literary expression, and Holmes's divergence from Emerson was revealed in the style of *Plato*. The essay proceeded methodically and chronologically and imposed a progressive character to the ideas discussed. Plato imposed system on Socrates's dialectic; subsequent philosophers furthered the development of systematic philosophy, just as natural scientists after Galileo added to knowledge of astronomy. The relation of past to present was established stylistically not by use of tense—Socrates and Plato speak most frequently in the present—but by Holmes's consistent contraposition of his subjects to the present narrator and reader through use of the editorial "we." He wrote, for example, that "Galileo's telescope, doubled, is our opera-glass" and that Plato "remains the original interpreter of certain primary facts and . . . still bears to us the same relation." Holmes as personal narrator—"I"—intruded only occasionally, but "I" appeared at the conclusion: "the spectacle, I say, of these two grand old heathen, the master the inspired fighter, the scholar the inspired thinker, fills my heart with love and reverence at one of the grandest sights the world can boast."

Holmes's classification of objects of knowledge in *Plato* suggested a rudimentary theory of knowledge by which he sought to harmonize aspects of idealism and empiricism by associating each with different intellectual activities. He sought to preserve the vitality of idealism for the limited but important area of art. Holmes stated that he intended that his criticism of idealist theory of complex ideas be true generally for both idealist and empiricist (sensationalist) perspectives.

His scheme did not adopt the Positivist hierarchy of sciences that Lewes promoted.[47] The Positivists organized sciences, understood as the knowledge of natural laws, in a descending series according to the simplicity or generality of the phenomena proper to the science—from astronomy to sociology. The autonomy of phenomena was

---

[46]Howe acknowledged the early essays' interest in empiricism, but he remarked that Holmes "rejected Platonism in metaphysics [but] accepted it in aesthetics." M. Howe, *supra* note 1, at 56. Emerson expressed his abiding appreciation for Plato in numerous places. His most sustained discussion was in *Representative Men* (1850), in 4 *The Collected Works of Ralph Waldo Emerson*, *supra* note 20, at 21.

[47]Holmes would have found the Positivist hierarchy set forth in 4 G. Lewes, *A Biolographical History of Philosophy, supra* note 43, at 258–61; G. Lewes, *Comte's Philosophy of the Sciences*, *supra* note 43, at 40–46.

fundamental to the Positivist scheme, and the Positivists excluded art and religion from their work, as they were neither sciences nor capable of being Positive—that is, capable of yielding knowledge of phenomena. Holmes's retention of art as a proper object of philosophical contemplation, requiring a place within a comprehensive classification, separated him from Positivism. His examples of simple and complex objects drawn from daily life had no correlation to proper objects of positive sciences and did not appear to reflect a Positivist influence. He further diverged from Positivism by emphasizing the basic similarity of artistic experience and factual knowledge. He wrote of the underlying identity of both real and ideal simple objects—the predicates of mathematical truth and "perhaps" beauty.

His concluding treatment of the advance of natural science since Galileo, and his critique of anachronistic reading of Plato, which he developed by analogy with the history of natural science, reflected a sense of progress. The passage has been isolated as evidence of a positivist or evolutionary influence, but the general vision of progress that Holmes embraced was shared by Emerson,[48] Whewell,[49] and many others in addition to Positivists.[50]

Holmes's belief that philosophy (or at least epistemology) could be made scientific undermined the continuing vitality of Plato's work. His progressive historical treatment of Plato challenged the utility of the sort of critical approach that he himself employed, and the judgment that Plato had little to contribute to contemporary philosophical study expressed also implicit criticism of both Emerson and Whewell.[51] The criticism revealed a profound change in attitude from the enthusiasm with which Holmes first embraced Emerson and approached Plato and that continued to surface in occasional bursts of praise. Holmes's efforts to defend the continuing importance of Plato by emphasizing his originality served to augment historical or biographical appreciation, but it did not provide an adequate ground for the continuing relevance of Plato's thought for systematic philosophy or science.

The essay's treatment of "science" reflected deep ambivalence and may help explain the origins of the ambiguous way that Holmes was

[48]R. Emerson, *Representative Men*, in 4 *The Collected Works of Ralph Waldo Emerson*, *supra* note 20, at 45.

[49]W. Whewell, *supra* note 44, at 347.

[50]G. Lewes, *A Biographical History of Philosophy*, *supra* note 43, at 248–50 (discussing the Positive theory of mental evolution).

[51]Whewell argued that, despite great progress in the history of sciences, no one since Plato had seriously addressed "the philosophical lesson to be derived from this progress" and that "new inferences remain to be drawn, of the nature of those which Plato drew." W. Whewell, *supra* note 44, at 353.

to use the term in his legal writings. On the one hand, science for him denoted intellectual disciplines or endeavors that generated positive knowledge by studying and classifying phenomena. On the other hand, science denoted formal or systematic attributes of a body of thought. The conflicting meanings led to inconsistent characterizations of Plato as "the scientific lecturer" and of the "loose and unscientific" nature of Plato's philosophy. The essay employed science in the following ways:

1. Plato was a "scientific" lecturer.
2. There was a beauty of the soul and a still higher beauty of "science."
3. "Science" founded on observation took a secondary place to Logic for Plato.
4. "Physical science" provided data for Logic.
5. The classification of Plato's system was "loose and unscientific."
6. Anachronistic valuations of Plato resulted from the "unscientific" neglect of the progress of thought.
7. Pythagorean doctrines were devoid of value because of the "entire absence of the central idea of science."
8. Plato's insight into nature was admirable if one abandoned the "exactness of science which Plato tried too early to attain."
9. Only in recent times an "all-comprehending science has embraced the universe" by demonstrating laws in all disciplines and generalizing all phenomena.

Most of these uses of the term did not distinguish between its reference to inherent attributes of a system of explanation or its reference to external fact-based methods of accumulating knowledge. Holmes used the term both in the sense that he found it used by classical philologists[52] and in the progressive naturalistic sense in which Emerson and the Positivists used it. While associating science with certain methods, he associated it above all with temporal sequence: Pythagoras was unscientific and of little value to present science, but so, too, was Galileo. Association of science with progress assumed a further standard for scientific development that Holmes did not make explicit. His ambivalent expressions comport with Positivist historical schemes in part; they comport also with Plato's differentiation of particular and ideal sciences—as explained by Ritter.[53]

Holmes's ambivalent treatment of "science" and evaluation of Plato do not indicate a conversion to Positivism. On the contrary, his

---

[52]*See* 2 H. Ritter, *The History of Ancient Philosophy* 189–95 (A. Morrison trans. 1838).

[53]*Id.*

treatment of Plato makes sense only in the context of his simultaneous efforts to develop a theory of art, which manifested continuing adherence to idealist epistemology and which defended transcendentalist aesthetics. He was able to embrace two inconsistent theories of knowledge because he associated each with different kinds of objects: idealism was proper for mathematics and art, whose objects were simple ideas; empiricism was proper for understanding the origin or truth of more mundane objects. Holmes avoided confronting the internal tensions between the two theories of knowledge by avoiding the elaboration of systematic philosophy. However, by expressing his views critically, in reaction to others, Holmes himself failed to attain the kind of scientific philosophy that he argued had eluded Plato.[54]

C. Art Philosophy

The problems that emerged in Holmes's treatment of the history of philosophy and "science" were closely related to his efforts to elaborate a philosophy of art. In turning to history of art, Holmes sought to escape the dilemma posed by the history of philosophy and science, for great works of art acquired intrinsic value that was independent of their historical context.

In the two articles *Notes on Albert Durer* [*sic*] and *Pre-Raphaelitism*, Holmes attempted to develop a systematic transcendentalist theory of art and to apply it to concrete works and movements. The essays were important for what they did not do: Holmes made no effort to relate his work in art to a comprehensive system of philosophy, nor did he dictate for art specific developmental norms of the kind the Positivists dictated for the mental evolution of sciences. On the contrary, he emphasized the ironic, nonprogressive character of the history of art. For example, he explained the artistic force of Dürer's work as a product of the backwardness of Dürer's times. Writing glowingly of Romantic abstract religion, Holmes, nonetheless, sensed the artistic loss that resulted from the decline of the religious force of images and stories.

A historical explanation of the origin of artistic impulse did not, however, account for the continuing power of religiously inspired art. To explain the artistic experience, Holmes adopted the transcendentalist understanding of art: art expressed spiritual truth in a concrete form that was communicated immediately to the observer. As evidence of the transcendental message and its

[54]Holmes announced in the article that he would discuss Plato's failure to develop a system elsewhere, but no such work has survived.

independence from what Holmes took to be backward faith, he pointed to the still greater power of some of Dürer's works with secular topics, like *Melancholy*.

While relating the greater effect of earlier religious art to the faith of the artist, Holmes did not explore the faith, the relation of faith to art, or the ritual aspects of earlier art. Rather, he sought to explore the power of Dürer's work through the technical methods of producing images, comparing Dürer's with modern methods. The discussion of method, with its unfavorable judgment of more recent artists,[55] reflected the reigning nostalgia of old and popular art; it rejected a progressive or evolutionary view of art history and expressed a Romantic association of the decline of art with the rise of science and civilization.

Both *Notes on Albert Durer* and *Pre-Raphaelitism* reflected the influence of Ruskin.[56] Holmes or another family member withdrew Ruskin's *Pre-Raphaelitism* and *Stones of Venice* from the library in 1858.[57] Before he entered Harvard, his parents had given him a copy of *Modern Painters*; during his first year at Harvard he bought *Elements of Drawing*, and his brother and sister gave him *Pre-Raphaelitism* and *The Political Economy of Art*.[58] Though his explicit reference to Ruskin in the college articles was often critical, his enthusiasm for Ruskin is evident from the depth of the influence, and Holmes in later years recalled his youthful enthusiasm for Ruskin.[59]

Ruskin's views, like Emerson's, were familiar to educated readers,[60] and explicit citation was unnecessary. The title of Holmes's last college article, *Pre-Raphaelitism*, was taken from the well-known polemical work by Ruskin.[61] Holmes acquired from Ruskin his great admiration for Dürer, which is evident. Ruskin had repeatedly

---

[55]Holmes's technical grasp of the media has been praised lavishly by some biographers, but their judgment is questionable. For example, several writers have described the essay as a discussion of Dürer's woodcuts when the prints that Holmes discussed at length were engravings not woodcuts. It does not take an expert to observe that Holmes's initial treatment of method (which discusses woodcut technique) was ineffectively related to his following discussion of particular works (most of which were not woodcuts).

[56]Ruskin's influence in antebellum America is discussed by R. Stein, *John Ruskin and Aesthetic Thought in America 1840–1900*, 1–146 (1967).

[57]*See* M. Howe, *supra* note 1, at 42–43.

[58]L. Baker, *supra* note 1, at 91.

[59]Letter to Sergeant, July 15, 1926, *quoted in* E. Sergeant, *supra* note 42. *See also* Holmes, *Address at Northwestern University Law School* (1902), in O. Holmes, *supra* note 13, at 275 (citing Ruskin).

[60]R. Stein observes, "By 1855 Ruskin felt that he had a more significant audience in America than in England." R. Stein, *supra* note 56, at 263.

[61]J. Ruskin, *Pre-Raphaelitism* (1851).

praised Dürer. *The Elements of Drawing* treated Dürer's work as a model and urged readers to obtain a print by the artist. One art critic has characterized Holmes's discussion of Dürer's technique as strikingly original,[62] but in fact Holmes's discussion of method derived from Ruskin, and Holmes's critical observations followed Ruskin closely. Emphasizing the importance of individual line, for example, Holmes wrote, "Thus it is, that, as I have said, we find with Durer every line is keen as the stroke of a surgeon's knife, not one superfluous, not one to be changed but with a corresponding change of effect." Holmes here followed Ruskin's emphasis on the importance of precision of line in Dürer,[63] and Holmes's language echoed Ruskin's words that "not a line nor dot [in Dürer] can be displaced without harm. . . . [A]ll add to the effect, and either express something, or illumine something, or relieve something."[64] Holmes followed Ruskin, too, in contrasting Dürer's precision to the woodcut illustrations in contemporary popular periodicals.

In relating the power of Dürer's art to his faith, Holmes also followed Ruskin. In the last volume of *Modern Painters*, Ruskin had become increasingly sensitive to the effect of religious beliefs on artistic expression. He had explained characteristics of Venetian art by the devout faith of the city, in contrast to the more worldly and abstract faith elsewhere in Italy,[65] and he had written generally of the Reformation's destruction of the possibility of simple, unquestioning faith and the resulting movement of artists to worldly themes.[66] Ruskin had identified Dürer as one of the great artists to oppose this trend, and he had focused on the allegorical treatments *Knight and Death*—"Der Reuter" (1513) now known as *Knight, Death, and Devil* [Plate 1]—and *Melancholy—Melencolia I* (1514) [Plate 2]—as works of religious faith and concrete representation that resisted

---

[62]Stechow, *supra* note 6, at 120. *See also* L. Baker, *supra* note 1, at 92 (quoting Stechow's judgment as authoritative). In making this judgment, however, Stechow ignored Ruskin's remarks about Dürer published in *The Elements of Drawing*.

[63]J. Ruskin, *The Elements of Drawing*, in 15 *The Works of John Ruskin* 79, 81–82, 85 (Lib. ed. 1904).

[64]*Id.* at 87.

[65]J. Ruskin, 5 *Modern Painters*, in 7 *The Works of John Ruskin*, at 288–89 (Lib. ed. 1905).

[66]*Id.* at 300–01.

PLATE 1. Albrecht Dürer, "Knight, Death, and Devil" (engraving 1513). *Harvey D. Parker Fund. Courtesy, Museum of Fine Arts, Boston.*

PLATE 2. Albrecht Dürer, "Melancolia I" (engraving 1514). Centennial gift of Landon T. Clay. *Courtesy, Museum of Fine Arts, Boston.*

the decline of faith and the artistic movement toward abstraction.[67] So, too, Holmes identified these specific works as among Dürer's greatest.

Ruskin's sensitivity to the force of religion in the last volume of *Modern Painters* was the outgrowth of personal experiences. It was closely intertwined with Ruskin's change of taste and growing personal appreciation of Dürer.[68] In a sense Holmes started at the point Ruskin had reached—deep personal appreciation of Dürer's art and concomitant appreciation of the religious impulse that generated it. But Holmes's emphasis on religious roots of artistic creation also reflected the pervasive interpretive gloss that Ruskin's theories received from American readers.[69] Holmes was not original in his effort to relate art to the naive faith of Dürer's days. Indeed, his historical understanding of that faith was less sophisticated than Ruskin's, for, unlike Ruskin, Holmes did not emphasize Dürer's conservative opposition to the challenges to faith posed by the Reformation. Emphasizing Dürer's conservative position would have

---

[67]I have adopted the dating of the engravings given by J. Hutchison, *Albrecht Dürer: A Biography* (1990).

Ruskin wrote that Dürer in *Knight, Death, and Devil* studied the question of death more deeply and gave more conclusive answers than any previous artist. J. Ruskin, 5 *Modern Painters*, 7 *The Works of John Ruskin*, *supra* note 65, at 306. He gave a problematic interpretation of the allegory. *Id.* at 310–11. He wrote in praise of *Melancolia I*, which he described but admitted that much of the symbolism eluded him. *Id.* at 312–13. Holmes, too, wrote that the symbolism was opaque. Ironically, Ruskin viewed the objects surrounding the central figure as symbols of labor, and Holmes viewed the objects more accurately as symbols of science, or "universal study"; neither viewed the objects, which include in prominent display woodworking tools as symbolizing art.

[68]The change of attitude towards Dürer was cause as much as consequence of Ruskin's sensitivity to the religious impulse of artistic production. In earlier volumes Ruskin had treated Dürer more coldly. He had characterized *Knight, Death, and Devil* as a noble example of grotesque art in volume three (1856). *See* J. Ruskin, 3 *Modern Painters*, 5 *The Works of John Ruskin* 131 (Lib. ed. 1904). He had written of the "absence of perception of the beautiful" in Dürer in volume 4 (1856). J. Ruskin, 4 *Modern Painters*, 6 *The Works of John Ruskin* 404 (Lib. ed. 1904). A brief account of some of the important formative experiences in the period between the fourth and last volume is set forth in Cook, *Introduction*, 7 *The Works of John Ruskin*, *supra* note 65. Ruskin also discussed them in the Preface to volume five and in later autobiographical writings. It seems likely, however, that his close study of Dürer's technique in connection with *Elements of Drawing* (1857) also increased his appreciation of Dürer's art.

[69]*See* R. Stein, *supra* note 56, at 84–100.

detracted from Holmes's polemical argument and his defense of abstract Romantic theology.

Holmes tried to further Ruskin's analysis in two ways. First, he tried to develop the theoretical grounds for a more comprehensive explanation of the ironic, nonprogressive history of culture. The decline of simple faith that made possible progress in "science" accounted equally for a regression in art; and philosophy, to be scientific in the broadest sense, must account for the irony. Holmes grasped the continuing value of past art, notwithstanding progress in science, as an analogy to justify the continuing merit of Plato and the critical study of past philosophy. Second, in elaborating a classification of Dürer's works, Holmes tried to develop a general system or science of classification for art.

In attempting to explain the power of art and its nonprogressive history and to organize systematically individual works and types, Holmes diverged from Ruskin. Taking *Melancholy* as typical of the highest achievement in art, Holmes implicitly challenged the historical explanation of Dürer's art as an expression of the artist's faith, for *Melancholy* was a classical allegory, lacking the topical Christian symbolism of *Knight, Death, and Devil*. Moreover, unlike Ruskin, Holmes had little interest in Dürer's realism. Holmes ranked the works according to their ideality or generality: "Highest would come such poems as the MELANCOLIA, which is as preferable to any scene or representation of a momentary fact as existence is higher than incident . . ." He ranked individual works in ascending order according to how effectively they represented the ideal:

Holmes's Hierarchy

Specific Works	Type	
		IDEAL–UNIVERSAL
Melancholy	imaginative representation of the ideal	
Knight, Death, and Devil; Resurrection *Bearing of the Cross* *Life of the Virgin*	imaginative representation of the ideal through exemplary individuals	
[No works]	less imaginative and more mundane subjects still lifes mere exercises	
		REAL–INDIVIDUAL

Lowest were unimaginative depictions of individual subjects—realistic, perhaps, but without symbolic value.

While much of Holmes's understanding of Dürer's work, technique, and historical context derived from Ruskin, the theory of art set forth in *Notes of Albert Durer* was a systematic elaboration of Emerson's ideas.[70] Emerson's theory rested on an idealist aesthetics that, in turn, derived from the German Romantics and Coleridge. For Emerson art communicated the ideal behind the image: "In a portrait, [the artist] must inscribe the character, and not the features, and must esteem the man who sits to him as himself only an imperfect picture or likeness of the aspiring original within."[71] Holmes adopted this idealist aesthetics and wrote:

> [T]he presumption is always in favor of that picture being greatest in which the lower truth of the individual is made subservient . . . to the

---

[70]Emerson had been publishing the chief features of his idealist theory of beauty and aesthetics for decades. Important books in which Emerson developed his theory of art and beauty and to which Holmes had access at or before the time he drafted his college essays included R. Emerson, *Nature* 28–30, 68–69 (1968) (facsimile of 1st ed. 1836); R. Emerson, *Essays: First Series*, in 2 *The Collected Works of Ralph Waldo Emerson* 209–18 (J. Slater, A. Ferguson, & J. Carr ed. 1979) (originally published 1841) (Essay XII: Art); *see also* R. Emerson, *The Conduct of Life* (1860), in *Ralph Waldo Emerson: Essays and Lectures* 937, 1104–12 (J. Porte ed. 1983). For aesthetic attitudes of Holmes's father, *see* [Holmes], *The Allston Exhibition*, 50 *N. Am. Rev.* 358–81 (1840).

Holmes was familiar with Emerson's important writings on the subject, but Emerson's influence cannot be limited to his writings. Emerson was active as a lecturer in Holmes's youth; he visited the Holmeses' home; and Holmes was doubtless present during conversations. Emerson's ideas were widely diffused among persons with whom Holmes had constant contact, including his father and father's friends.

Holmes had personal conversations with Emerson during his college years and gave Emerson a copy of *Plato*. Holmes later recalled these conversations in discussions and correspondence with Elizabeth Sergeant and others. *See* Holmes's letters to Sergeant, July 15 and December 7, 1926. Oliver Wendell Holmes, Jr. Papers, *supra* note 6, reel 37 (Howe's copies of the originals in Sergeant's possession); E. Sergeant, *supra* note 42, at 315–16. Howe suggests that the conversations occurred in Holmes's junior year based on the dates that *Plato* was withdrawn from the library. M. Howe, *supra* note 1, at 54. Baker treats them as occurring immediately upon Holmes's completion of the essay, in the summer between his junior and senior years. L. Baker *supra* note 1, at 90. For a study of the intellectual relation between Emerson and Holmes, *see* F. Mellen, Jr., Ralph Waldo Emerson, Justice Holmes, Modern American Law (unpublished M.A. thesis, University of Kentucky, 1971).

[71]*See* R. Emerson, *Essays: First Series*, *supra* note 70, at 209.

> profounder truth of the idea. [H]igher than anything connected with the individual is the conception of the harmonious whole of a great work, and this again is great, just as its idea partakes of what is eternal. And this striving to look on types and eternal ideas, is that highest gift of the artist, which is called the ideal tendency.

His classification represented an effort to elaborate a detailed system from general tenets of transcendentalism. The power of art to portray the ideal and universal accounted for its greatness; that power accounted also for the survival of art independent of historical context and explained the nonprogressive character of art history.

The typology reflected Holmes's personal taste,[72] but it also incorporated specific aesthetic criteria found in Emerson and represented a fundamental critique of Ruskin and the Pre-Raphaelite program. Ruskin's naturalism was complex and laden with fruitful inconsistencies. It had changed over time, revealing change in Ruskin's taste and attitude toward nature. Art for Ruskin remained strictly representational in the sense that nature must discipline the imagination and limit the scope of creative work. He suggested that children be given colors to play with: "If it [a child] merely daubs the paper with shapeless stains, the colour-box may be taken away till it knows better; but as soon as it begins painting red coats on soldiers,

---

[72]Holmes continued especially to admire Dürer's *Melancolia I* and *Knight, Death, and Devil*. Framed copies of both hung in his sitting room at his death. *See* The Oliver Wendell Holmes, Jr. Papers, *supra* note 6, reel 17.

For young Holmes, the greatest art was in the past. He appeared dissatisfied with, and uninterested in, contemporary art, though he voiced hope about future art. For him, prints represented a high art form. He was drawn to neither naturalism nor primitivism, and nonrepresentational art would challenge fundamentally his paradigm of art. His tastes may have reflected his childhood exposure to his father's print collection; at the same time, the subjects of prints stimulated his imagination for far away places. *See* L. Baker, *supra* note 1, at 91.

His tastes in later years remained remarkably close to those he expressed at college. He continued to admire Dürer and collected his work. *See* 1 O. Holmes, *Holmes-Laski Letters* 495, 561, 609, 713 (M. Howe ed. 1953); 2 *Holmes-Pollock Letters*, *supra* note 17, at 156; *Justice Holmes to Dr. Wu*, *supra* note 14, at 11. His interest in lineal representation was reflected in sketches and maps that he made during the war. *See generally* O. Holmes, *Touched with Fire*, *supra* note 8, illustrations. He bequeathed his extensive collection of 670 lithographs, engravings, etchings, prints, and drawings to the Library of Congress. They were valued at over $7,000 at his death. *See* The Oliver Wendell Holmes, Jr. Papers, *supra* note 6, reel 17. His extensive collection of cartoons also evinced the appeal of representations with an identifiable message. The Oliver Wendell Holmes, Jr. Papers, *supra* note 6, reels 62 & 63.

striped flags to ships, etc., it should have colours at its command."[73] As to depiction of nature, Ruskin was famous for championing the work of Turner and recent artists and for challenging neoclassical conventions; he urged artists at the end of the first volume of *Modern Painters* "to go to nature . . . having no other thought but how best to penetrate her meaning; rejecting nothing, selecting nothing, and scorning nothing." He celebrated the Pre-Raphaelites for putting his program into practice.[74]

In contrast, Holmes criticized the lack of an explicit criterion of selection in the works of Pre-Raphaelites: "Art involves in its very nature *selection*. . . . [W]e may doubt whether the present works [of the school] have the right to be called the fruits of art in its highest sense of all." The principle of selection had been central to neoclassical aesthetic theory, and Holmes appeared conservative in his attack on Ruskin and the Pre-Raphaelites. Holmes did not mean to defend convention; rather, he followed Emerson's view that art was inherently selective and creative. Selection applied both to subject[75] and to the representation of the subject, and abstraction and symbolism promoted the idealizing goals that the transcendentalists ascribed to art. Emerson exhorted, "[T]he details, the prose of nature, [the artist] should omit, and give us only the spirit and splendor."[76] Selection, by removing the contingent and idiosyncratic, represented the object and idealized the object by revealing the object's relation to the universal ideal. In contrast, Holmes ranked realistic depictions of contingent phenomena that lacked symbolic value to portray the ideal at the very bottom of his classification.

Holmes's vigorous defense of selection in revealing the ideal reinvigorated the transcendentalist doctrine that he had questioned in his treatment of the progress of philosophy in *Plato*. He did not explore the underlying grounds that made the typic, the ideal, beautiful in its appeal to the individual. Rather he sought to develop a system of classification for art, representing an effort to make transcendentalism scientific.

Holmes distinguished science and art according to properties of their respective subject matters. Philosophy in the narrow sense was

---

[73]J. Ruskin, *The Elements of Drawing*, 15 *The Works of John Ruskin*, *supra* note 63, at 9.

[74]*See* J. Ruskin, *Pre-Raphaelitism*, *supra* note 61, at 5. Ruskin and the Pre-Raphaelites had independent origins and differed in important ways, and Ruskin later distanced himself from some of the Pre-Raphaelites that he had initially championed.

[75]"In all design, art lies in making your object prominent, but there is a prior art in choosing objects that are prominent." R. Emerson, *The Conduct of Life*, *supra* note 70, at 1106.

[76]R. Emerson, *Essays: First Series*, *supra* note 70, at 209.

scientific and was characterized by progressive elaboration of results. In a more comprehensive sense, however, true philosophy must embrace art and explicate the nonprogression of the ideal: "The ideal spirit may be influenced by circumstances, but it is the great gift of humanity, not of a sect; it inspired the philosopher Plato, the artist among thinkers, as well as the Christian Durer, a thinker among artists." Nevertheless, Holmes's critical conclusions ultimately contradicted the vision of reconciling art and science in a comprehensive art philosophy.

He expressed his dissatisfaction with contemporary art and philosophy of art in *Pre-Raphaelitism*. Combining Ruskin's criticism with Emerson's metaphysics, he sought to evaluate the art actually produced by the Pre-Raphaelites. The essay contrasted with *Notes on Albert Durer*, however, in its lack of discussion of specific works or artists. He referred directly to only one work in the article, and he did not mention a single Pre-Raphaelite artist by name, alluding only generally to art produced by the school.

Holmes attributed the failure of Pre-Raphaelite art to its academic program; the strong implication of the essay was that great art could not be wilfully produced by application of an abstract theory of art. On the contrary, Holmes had emphasized that Dürer's force lay just in his naive faith and lack of reflection.

In turning to art, Holmes avoided grappling with the impasse that he had reached in his critical treatment of the history of philosophy. But in art theory, too, he reached an impasse. Neither the historical age of faith nor its corresponding simple powerful artistic products could be arbitrarily reproduced academically. On the one hand, Plato's philosophic weaknesses lay in his failure to attain science. On the other hand, Ruskin and the Pre-Raphaelites failed to regenerate art because of their academic program. Art deterred science; science deterred art. The vision of comprehensive art philosophy reconciling science and art remained an unattained ideal. The ideal was pushed off to the future in the conclusion of *Pre-Raphaelitism*, and criticism in art, as in philosophy, served only to demonstrate the unreality of the vision. The partisan and ironic appreciation of history emphasized the gulf between real and ideal without demonstrating how the two might be reconciled.

CHAPTER 3

Search for Control

JEROME FRANK provided mythic foundation for the view that Holmes broke radically with philosophical and legal tradition. Frank described Holmes in psychoanalytic language as the modern jurist who "has put away childish longings for a father controlled world."[1] Plentiful evidence of Holmes's tension with his father tempted biographers to emphasize generational conflict, which, in turn, supported interpretations that emphasized his novelty and discontinuity.[2]

Holmes's inner conflicts have invited psychological explanations for over a century. William James observed in 1869 that Holmes "amuses me by being composed of at least two and a half different people rolled into one, and the way he keeps them together in one tight skin, without quarreling any more than they do, is remarkable."[3] But Holmes promised to be a particularly poor subject for psychological study. Not much evidence survived from critical periods in his personal growth.[4] And psychological biographies were frustrated by the fact that Holmes censored the record by destroying

---

[1]J. Frank, *Law and the Modern Mind* 253 (1931).

[2]*See generally* White, *Holmes's "Life Plan": Confronting Ambition, Passion, and Powerlessness*, 65 *N.Y.U.L. Rev.* 1409, 1413–18 (1990) (discussing recent biographies).

[3]Letter to Henry P. Bowditch, May 22, 1869, 1 R. Perry, *The Thought and Character of William James* 297 (1936).

[4]Recent biographers have speculated about private aspects of Holmes's life. Even if details of his private life were appropriate subjects for biography, it is obvious from the conflicting speculations that the evidence is inconclusive. *See* L. Baker, *The Justice From Beacon Hill: The Life and Times of Oliver Wendell Holmes* 220 (1991) (allusions to possible visits to prostitutes), *id.* at 229 (speculation about impotency and consummation of marriage); S. Novick, *Honorable Justice: The Life of Oliver Wendell Holmes* 102 (1989) (allusion by "subtext" to homoerotic attraction to or homosexual relationship with Henry James), *id.* at 188 (speculation about extramarital affairs with Lucy Clifford and Lady Castletown).

revealing documents.[5] The material that survived may have been misleading in important ways.[6]

Nevertheless, a partial psychological reconstruction is possible, and a psychoanalytically informed intellectual biography corrects or supplements some of the biographical treatments. Contrary to biographical lore of his early childhood strife with his father—for which the evidence is thin—Holmes actually manifested a late but enduring pattern of personal competition with his father. A careful examination of the evidence of his relationship with his father ultimately contradicts Jerome Frank's theory that Holmes overcame the urge for parental dominance.

A psychoanalytic approach to Holmes's development suggests that the emotional energy behind his fight against natural law had deep roots. From a psychoanalytic perspective, his intellectual activity and the content of his theory emerge as expressions of his unresolved struggle with ideas associated with his father. Above all, Holmes's life and ideas were marked by efforts to control conflict; yet he sought to avoid or resolve conflict neither in his life nor in his theory. Rather he sought to play with conflict and control in his personal life, and he worked to perpetuate and repeat conflict by incorporating it as a distinctive feature of legal theory.

A. The Oedipus

The mystery of Holmes's early relationship with his parents is only increased by the glimpse of a childhood memory. At age seventy, in association with reflections about his death, he recalled: "I remember getting the same impression as a little boy . . . from the cover of my copy of Jack and the Beanstalk. The beanstalk was cut off

---

[5]The practice of self-censorship began with documents generated during the war. Holmes continued to destroy documents throughout his life. Writing to Lewis Einstein in 1932, he commented on a recent biography: "I have not read it, but I should think it was harmless. I had nothing to do with it. Perhaps when I die my executor . . . may do something with more materials, but I have done my best to destroy illuminating documents." *The Holmes-Einstein Letters: Correspondence of Mr. Justice Holmes and Lewis Einstein 1903–1935* 349 (J. Peabody ed. 1964).

[6]For example, Baker characterizes his war letters as unemotional. L. Baker, *supra* note 4, at 106, 111. But the letters that survive may not be representative, for Holmes may have destroyed those that expressed his feelings, especially if he later viewed them with shame or embarrassment.

At the same time that Holmes *selectively* destroyed material in his possession, there is good reason to question the sincerity with which he urged his correspondents to destroy his letters. *See* L. Baker, *supra* note 4, at 17–18.

by the top of the cover and Jack was climbing—to one could not see what mysterious end. The picture has stuck by me through life."[7]

When he was twenty months, his mother or father recorded his limited vocabulary in a memorandum. At that age he knew names of one object (milk), one activity (walk), three directional adverbs (out, in, off), and an expression of approval (all well). He knew four personal names: "Auber" (Oliver), "[H]enny" (Wendy), "Aahma" (grandma), and "Mamy" (Mary).[8] The baby knew his nurse's name but did not yet know his parents' names. As he learned to say "almost anything" over the next few months, he learned to address his father and mother as "faver and mover."[9]

Nothing is known of the role of the nurse in raising Holmes nor of the baby's relations with his mother. Evidence from much later in Holmes's life suggests that he may have suffered an early, painful separation from his mother. He remembered reacting with terror to an older boy's joking remark, "See you when your mother is hung," which caused him to believe his mother would be killed.[10] His need for oral gratification remained intense, and he associated objects of oral stimulation with his identity as an adult. In sketches that he drew of himself, he depicted himself with a pipe [Plates 3 and 4]. He smoked off and on for much of his life and recorded dates of attempts to quit pipe smoking.[11] Quitting proved difficult and caused him insomnia.[12]

Early events that affected his relation to his parents included the birth of his sister when he was two and of his brother when he was

---

[7]Letter of October 14, 1911 to Alice S. Green, The Oliver Wendell Holmes, Jr. Papers (University Publications of America, 1985) (Microfilm Project), reel 32. *Quoted in part in* S. Novick, *supra* note 4, at 10.

[8]Manuscript note, "20 Months—Wendy," Oliver Wendell Holmes, Sr., Papers, The Houghton Library, Harvard University. The manuscript note is included in a scrapbook which includes material from 1860. Howe discusses attribution of the manuscript. M. Howe, *Justice Oliver Wendell Holmes: The Shaping Years* 289 n.4 (1957).

[9]Manuscript note, "26 Months," Oliver Wendell Holmes, Sr., Papers, Houghton Library, Harvard University.

[10]Holmes related the story to Charles P. Curtis, Jr., who related it to Bowen. C. Bowen, *Yankee from Olympus: Justice Holmes and His Family* 93–94, 436, 439 (1944).

[11]*Cf.* Diary entries for January 17, 1871 and July 21–22, 1891 in Little, *The Early Reading of Oliver Wendell Holmes*, 7 *Harv. Library Bull.* 182 (1954), and Black Book, Oliver Wendell Holmes, Jr., Papers, Harvard Law School Library, at 151, col. 2. *See generally* S. Novick, *supra* note 4, at 120.

[12]Henry James wrote in his *Autobiography* 532 (1956): "How does Mr. Holmes persevere about smoking? I pity him if he can't sleep, and I wish I had a vicious habit so that I might give it up."

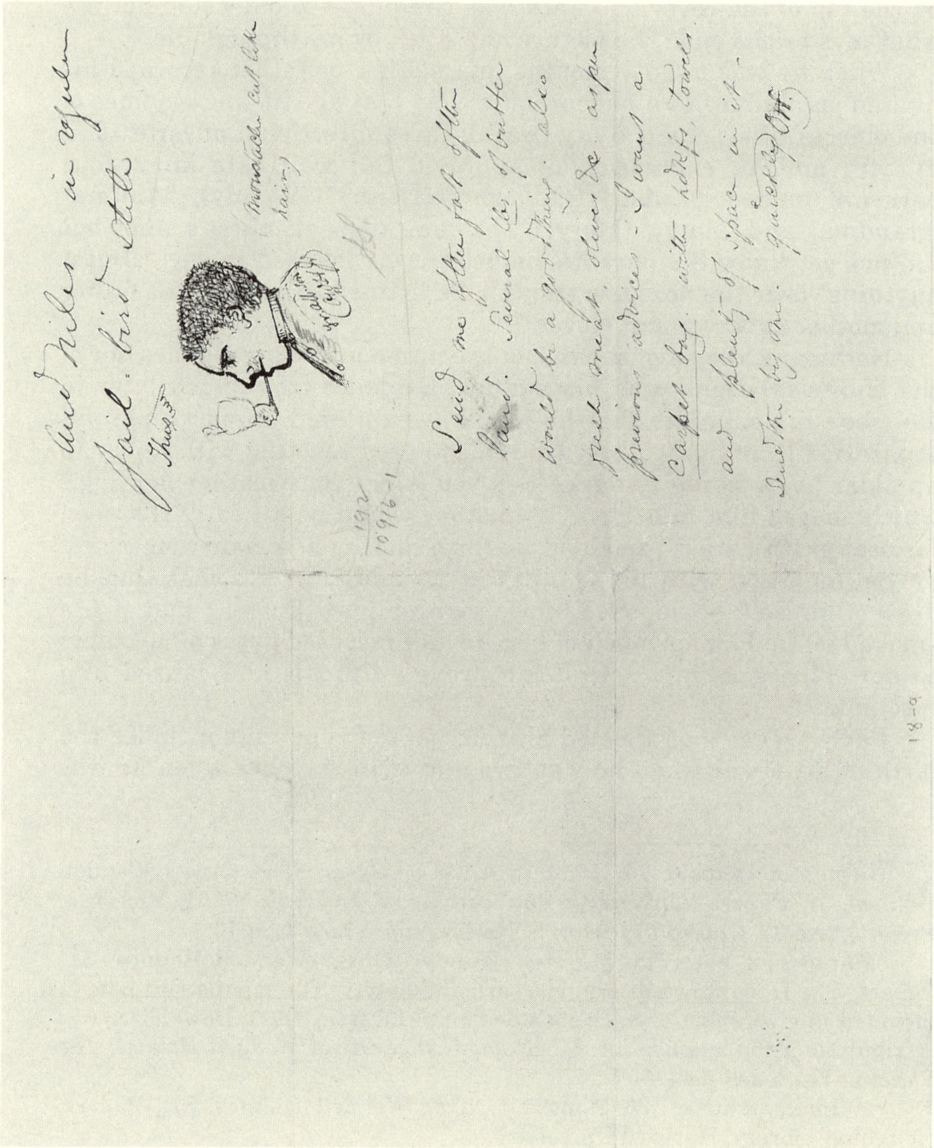

PLATE 3. Holmes self-portrait sketch, in letter of May 1, 1861. *Harvard Law School Library.*

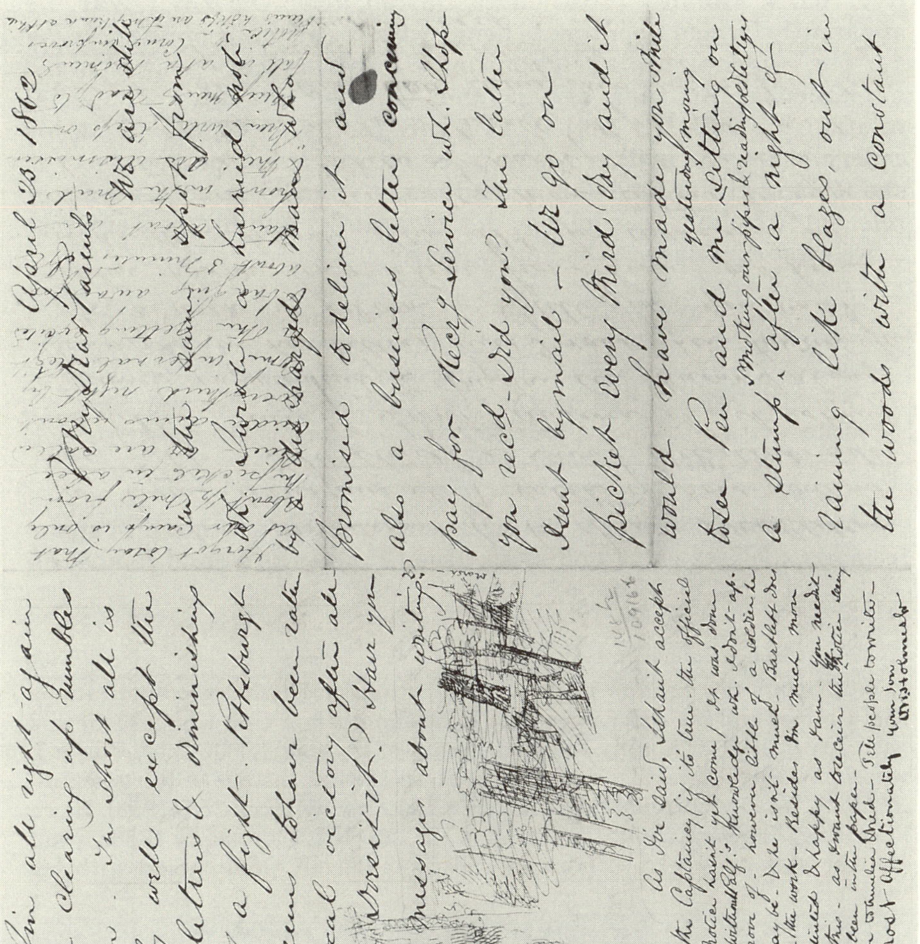

PLATE 4. Holmes self-portrait sketch, in letter of April 23, 1862. *Harvard Law School Library.*

five. When Holmes returned to Boston after the Civil War, he apparently formed no intimate bonds with his sister or brother.[13]

The evidence of his relationship with his mother stems from his adolescence. At that age Holmes seemed to enjoy a special relationship with his mother. In a rare family photograph from his college years, his mother seems to be returning his fond gaze—or is she looking at her husband, seated next to him?[14] In 1866 his sister referred to Holmes teasingly as the "favorite."[15] And his mother wrote to welcome him back to the family house:

> What does a woman of my age care as much for as her children—what they are, what they will be—I assure you that I give more thought to them than to anything else in this world—Yes dear Wendell, you will find me the same fond mother when you come home that I was when I bade you goodbye—I suppose I bother you sometimes—but I love you very much—[16]

Most of the evidence of his relationship with his father also stems from his adolescence. Familiar stories of Holmes as a child competing

---

[13]Though few records survive, Howe writes: "[T]here are no indications that Holmes and his sister were close to one another, or that Holmes followed with any special sympathy the misfortunes of his younger brother, Edward, whose ill health . . . ended with his death in 1884 at the age of thirty-eight." M. Howe, *Justice Oliver Wendell Holmes: The Proving Years* 255 (1963). Howe is writing, however, about the period in the late 1870s and early 1880s when Holmes was intensely withdrawn and compulsively preoccupied with his work.

[14]*See* the portrait in S. Novick, *supra* note 4, facing page 266.

[15]*See* L. Baker, *supra* note 4, at 181. This reference has been identified as evidence that he was the family favorite, but in fact his sister plainly meant that he was her favorite, for she closed the letter "Your loving and favorite sister." The Oliver Wendell Holmes, Jr. Papers, *supra* note 7, reel 33.

[16]Letter of Amelia Lee Jackson Holmes to Holmes dated July 22, 1866, quoted in S. Novick, *supra* note 4, at 94. Novick treats this letter in the context of Holmes's decision to return home from the war two years earlier, and he includes several other letter from his mother from the summer of 1866 in his treatment of Holmes's childhood. *Id.* at 15.

The force of emotion expressed in this letter as well as the need to express it may be cause for questioning its apparent meaning. In other letters, his mother expressed some relief when Holmes left the house. "Wendell has gone to Mrs. Brooks's for a few days, and I am quite glad of it." Letter of August 5 [?] to Emily, in The Oliver Wendell Holmes, Jr. Papers, *supra* note 7, reel 33. "Wendell went into the country last Tuesday and I have been making the most of my time since." Letter of Sunday, June 14, [1863], in *id.*

intensely with his father are largely fiction.[17] The surviving sources reveal hints of later insubordinate behavior only to the most penetrating hindsight. True, a school report from 1847 complained that he "talks too much."[18] Yet a letter of introduction from 1851 (when he was nine) described him as "uniformly docile, thoughtful, amiable and affectionate. Young as he is, his habits of application are confirmed."[19]

---

[17]For example, Novick writes that Holmes's father imposed strict discipline on his children and bullied Holmes. S. Novick, *supra* note 4, at 10, 14. *See also* G. Aichele, *Oliver Wendell Holmes, Jr.: Soldier, Scholar, Judge* 24 (1989). Pursing the sources that inspired such accounts either leads to fiction, to much later statements whose temporal references are inconclusive, or to autobiographical remarks that may reveal hostility that manifested itself later in Holmes's life.

Howe suggested that Holmes and his brother expressed childish hostility toward their father based on an entry in Alice James diary. M. Howe, *supra* note 8, at 11–12. The evidence is a passage in the diary of Alice James (invalid sister of William and Henry James) that she entered in 1888:

> I remember Father coming home one Saturday from the dinner [of the Saturday Club] and telling, among other things, that Dr. Holmes had asked if he did not find that his sons despised him and seemed surprised when F[ather] said no, that he was not oppressed in that way.—"But after all, it is only natural they should, for they stand upon our shoulders," exclaimed the Doctor, a truly dizzy height for the accomplished and elongated Wendell! The figure immediately presents itself of the two a la church steeple.

A. James, *The Diary of Alice James* 69 (L. Edel ed. 1964). But there is reason to question whether this memory (even if accurate) related to Holmes's *childhood*. His father's interest in psychiatric phenomena waxed in the late 1880s when he incorporated psychological theories in his novels (1858, 1867, 1885) and other writings, some of which anticipated Freud. But it is unlikely that this incident later recorded by Alice James occurred before Holmes was in college. It is still more unlikely that the incident occurred earlier than Holmes's adolescent years because Alice James was born in 1848. It is implausible that a child under ten would have been present during or would have remembered the remarks she later recalled.

Moveover, if her additional remarks about Holmes's height and accomplishments related to her associations upon first hearing the statement, its probable date would be still later, for his earliest accomplishments that she would have known would have occurred during the Civil War. At that time she was in her teens and the Saturday Club was still meeting. Such a date comports with the analysis I suggest for Holmes's relations with his father during and after college.

[18]"Report of Recitations and Deportment for the week ending 19 June 1847," Oliver Wendell Holmes, Jr., Papers, Harvard Law School Library, Manuscript Box 69, Folder 1.

[19]Letter of J.R. Sullivan to E.S. Dixwell (Holmes' instructor and future father-in-law) of September 29, 1851, Oliver Wendell Holmes, Jr., Papers,

Although biographical reconstructions of Holmes's early childhood and youth are largely works of art, a good deal is known of his early adult development. By his first year in college he had closely followed his celebrated father's steps in choice of college (Harvard), philosophy (transcendentalism), religion (Unitarianism). He had the same name as his father. His handwriting looked like his father's. Lanky, with a long straight nose and deep-set eyes, he looked strikingly like a taller version of his father. At the end of college he, like his father, was class poet.

Duplication of his father's experiences was so extensive that it has attracted little critical attention. Biographers have written with the assumption that he was predestined to follow his father's steps. "It was unthinkable for Wendell Holmes of Boston to have gone anywhere but Harvard."[20]

His father's fame undoubtedly increased the opportunity for him to follow his father's steps on occasions like reciting class poems.[21] Holmes's caste provided expectations and opportunities for him to attend Harvard. It is no less significant that Holmes took full advantage of such opportunities. And it may be especially significant that he did so without apparent reflection or choice. The lack of choice that makes such events of little interest to traditional biography is all the more astonishing because it is accepted as normal, requiring no further explanation on an intuitive level.

Holmes's conformity to his father also expressed itself intellectually. His college writings revealed his enthusiasm for transcendentalist philosophy. In fact, he was propounding an extreme form of transcendentalism at the very moment that Comte's positivism was becoming debated within Unitarian circles and gaining acceptance among the young thinkers in New England.[22]

Harvard Law School Library, Manuscript Box 69, Folder 2 (mounted with border decorated by Holmes' wife and the addressee's daughter).

[20]L. Baker, *supra* note 4, at 72. *See also* C. Bowen, *supra* note 10, at 93, 115.

[21]O. Holmes, *Alma Mater*, 7 *The Harvard Magazine* 48 (1860). Senior poem 1861 (lost), discussed in M. Howe, *supra* note 8, at 75–76.

[22]Richard Laurin Hawkins discusses the spread of positivism and the negative reaction of Holmes's college teacher Professor Bowen. R. Hawkins, *Positivism in the United States* (1853–1861) 23–26, 36–39 (1938). Holmes's college essays reveal that he had read work by the positivist-influenced writer Lewes. O. Holmes, *Notes on Albert Durer, The Harvard Magazine* 41–47 (1860). But his college writings do not advocate positivism and continue to reveal the influence of transcendentalism. Goldsmith, arguing for direct influence of Holmes's father's theory on Holmes's mature thought, neglects the shift in Holmes's views and mistakenly associates his father's

Because of his adolescent assimilation of his father's ideas, Holmes's struggle to achieve individuality and to resolve tensions at the root of his identification with his father would influence the course of his intellectual biography. His mature philosophy and legal theory were the result of a critical engagement with and rejection of key ideas that derived from his father. The intellectual transformation that provided the context for his later theory was the intellectual expression of a more general breakdown of his early adult identification with his father.

Imitation of his father manifested a common psychological process that psychoanalytic theory explains as part of the Oedipus conflict. With adolescence there is normally a resurgence of the Oedipus conflict. Identification with an adult male plays a role in the resolution of the complex signaling a displacement of erotic drives: the adolescent behaves like his father in order to reproduce—with another woman—the father's relation with his mother.[23] Holmes's intense identification went far beyond the usual competitive posturing of adolescence, revealing, on the one hand, unresolved erotic drives for his mother, and, on the other hand, a defense or reaction formation to aggressive drives toward his father. By displacing and blending features of his own self with those of his father, Holmes also turned the aggression toward his father inward.[24]

It is clear that despite the extreme form of Holmes's identification, it did not effectively control or resolve underlying conflict with his father. The identification began to deteriorate before the Civil War, but the deterioration did not start at the highest intellectual levels. Holmes continued to identify strongly with his father's moral and intellectual views in college. Though his college writings evidenced some interest in the new theory of Comte, he sought to accommodate aspects of the new theory to transcendentalist

---

transcendentalist novels with positivist psychology. *See* Goldsmith, *Oliver Wendell Holmes: Father and Son*, 48 J. *Crim. L. & Criminology* 394 (1957).

[23]The theoretical explanation of the process of identification is complex. Freud's views changed over time, and he may have accepted the existence of two different types of identification. *See generally* Compton, *The Concept of Identification in the Works of Freud, Ferenczi, and Abraham*, 54 *Psychoanalytic Q.* 200, 200–33 (1985). Some psychoanalysts have classed it as a defense mechanism—*e.g.*, W. Toman, *An Introduction to Psychoanalytic Theory of Motivation* 40–44 (1960).

[24]The intensity of identification is related to loss of an object. Where the identification is with a competitor, the intensity derives from the loss of the loved object. Consequently, Holmes's intense adolescent identification with his father would be completely consistent with an early separation from his mother and childhood fantasy of her death. *See* Compton, *supra* note 23, at 220.

philosophy. Only at the end of college did Holmes announce his intention of going to law school: "If I survive the war I expect to study law as my profession or at least for a starting point."[25] Only at the end of college was he interested in Hobbes and Austin.[26]

Deterioration of the identification was expressed nonintellectually by petty criminal and destructive acts. Holmes was fined one dollar for defacing the posts in a tutor's room; he was admonished for participating in a disturbance; he was admonished for "gross indecorum" during class; he was fined ten dollars for breaking windows of an underclassman.[27] Holmes's acts all expressed hostility toward the school authority; they manifested aggressive urges that were directed specifically against authority figures—the tutor, the professor, and the college property. This destructive and rebellious behavior revealed his inability to contain the underlying hostility, which was redirected toward school property and personnel—substituted paternal authority. His conflicting feelings toward his father were reflected in his attitude toward the college: for all the animosity revealed in his behavior as a student, in later years "he remained intensely loyal to the institution."[28]

His writings in college reflected his ambivalent relation to paternal authority. He ridiculed academic views and moral attitudes that he associated with the college, and he defended, or at least tolerated, student rowdyism. But he also chided fellow students for their immaturity. His philosophical perspective and even his style derived from contemporaries of his father, especially Emerson and Ruskin. Like Emerson, Holmes's father was critical of the Harvard orthodoxy, and Holmes's rebellion was fostered at high intellectual levels by the object against which it was unconsciously directed.

Channeling hostility towards college authority was encouraged and reinforced by his father, and his father's conduct may have been influenced by the fear of repeating his own traumatic college experience, when a generation before he had identified with liberal religious views against which his minister father had crusaded.[29] It is

---

[25]O. Holmes, *Autobiographical Sketch*, in *Mind and Faith of Justice Holmes* 8 (M. Lerner ed. 1946).

[26]M. Howe, *supra* note 8, at 76–77.

[27]*See* L. Baker, *supra* note 4, at 81–82; M. Howe, *supra* note 8, at 38, 45, 62, 69.

[28]L. Baker, *supra* note 4, at 93.

[29]*See* E. Hoyt, *The Improper Bostonian: Dr. Oliver Wendel Holmes* 32–36 (1979). Holmes's father remembered the trauma caused by his early exposure to and subsequent rejection of Calvinist demonology.

> No child can overcome these early impressions without doing violence to the whole mental and moral machinery of his being. He may conquer them in later years, but the wrenches and strains

curious to observe that Holmes's father's novels traced adult neuroses and personality characteristics to infantile or prenatal traumas suffered by individuals who were motherless or orphaned.[30]

The outbursts of Holmes's aggressive behavior in college and the iconoclastic spirit of his writings revealed that the mechanics of identification did not effectively contain underlying aggressive feelings toward his father. His tentative career choice at the end of college and his new interest in Hobbes and Austin at that time also indicate a more conscious concern with the control of aggressiveness.[31] The selection of a career different from his father, the interest in anti-idealist philosophers, and the growing intellectual independence reflected in his last college writings—all show that the breakdown in identification was shaping the content of his theorizing. ?

Holmes's physical appearance during the war years signaled the end of the identification. In earlier portraits Holmes looked remarkably like his clean-shaven father. He first sported a thin mustache sometime between April 1862 and January 1864, and he retained the mustache, grooming it ever more luxuriantly, until his death[32] [Plates 3, 4, 5, and Frontispiece].

> which his victory has cost him leave him a cripple as compared with a child trained in sound and reasonable beliefs. I had long passed into middle age before I could analyze the effect of these conflicting agencies.

The Autobiographical Notes, in 1 O. Holmes [Sr.], *Life and Letters of Oliver Wendell Holmes* 39–40 (J. Morse ed. 1896). *See also id.* at 43.

[30]*See* C. Obendorf, *The Psychiatric Novels of Oliver Wendell Holmes*, 22, 200–02 (2d ed. 1943) (reprint 1971).

[31]Holmes's biography confirms Dr. Watson's contemporary observation that persons who select a legal career evidence "an increased concern over the expression and nonexpression of aggressiveness." Watson, *The Quest for Professional Competence: Psychological Aspects of Legal Education*, 37 *U. of Cincinnati L. Rev.* 101 (1968). *See also* Watson, *Some Psychological Aspects of the Trial Judge's Decision-Making*, 39 *Mercer L. Rev.* 393 (1988).

[32]*Compare* M. Howe, *supra* note 8, plates 6, 7, 13 and 1 *Holmes-Pollock Letters: The Correspondence of Mr. Justice Holmes and Sir Frederick Pollock 1874–1932* 10 plate opposite (M. Howe ed. 1941). Holmes's self-portrait sketch in his May 1, 1861, letter to his mother depicts a stubble on his lip and a clean-shaven chin. The sketch has a note "moustache cut like hair." *See* O. Holmes, *Touched with Fire: Civil War Letters and Diary* 3 (M. Howe ed. 1946). His self self-portrait sketch in his letter of April 28, 1862 depicts him as cleanshaven. *See id.* at 45. Both self-portraits depict Holmes smoking a pipe (*see* illustrations, pages 58–59).

PLATE 5. Young Holmes. Portrait from early 1860s. *Harvard Law School Art Collection.*

PLATE 6. Holmes's mother and father. *Harvard Law School Art Collection.*

B. War

Holmes was committed to pro-Union antislavery politics in college. At the outbreak of the Civil War in his senior year, he eagerly enlisted and then sought a commission in the Twentieth Regiment of Massachusetts Volunteer Infantry. His smoldering disciplinary disputes with the college authorities ended with his move to camp and eventual graduation.

The context within which Holmes moved from Harvard to service, and soon to combat, suggests that war provided an outlet for powerful hostility that even at college had not been contained. His letters from the front communicate his eagerness to engage in combat and his disappointment in delays.[33] Entry into the war thus indicates a further deterioration of the identification; yet once again his father and mother encouraged the direction in which the aggression was directed, for Holmes shared Unionist convictions with his parents and was fulfilling their expectations by going to war.

Breakdown of identification does not fully explain Holmes's entry into the war. His motives for joining the war were complex[34] and overdetermined, but in seeking military experience as an outlet for aggressive feelings toward his father, the external manifestation of the hostility reflected the ultimate failure of the process of identification to channel and restrain the hostility.

Acknowledging the complexity of Holmes's motives for joining the war and seeking combat detracts neither from his conscious quest for valor nor from his political commitment to the abolitionist and Union cause.[35] Nor does it fully explain the psychological context of his war experience. Understanding independent sources of his aggressive impulses would be important for assessing the depth of his exhaustion at the end of the war.[36] But the deterioration of the identification helps explain the critical biographical problem of his subsequent disenchantment with the war and his decision to muster out before the war's end. It explains the source of the open conflicts with his father that broke out repeatedly during the war.

[33]*See* O. Holmes, *Touched with Fire*, *supra* note 32, at 8, 9–10, 43.

[34]*See generally*, M. Howe, *supra* note 8, at 71; L. Baker, *supra* note 4, at 97, 108–09.

[35]His hatred of slavery did not abate after the war. *See* M. Howe, *supra* note 8, at 70.

[36]Holmes left the war in a state of great fatigue and may actually have been suffering a war-induced neurosis. For years after the war he suffered various complaints, such as partial paralysis, that were aggravated by stress and that may have been symptoms of hysteria.

Howe first recognized that Holmes experienced a personal crisis during the war. Howe believed that the resolution of the crisis deeply influenced Holmes's mature philosophical perspective. He related Holmes's growing disenchantment with the war to "Copperhead" influences, and he isolated Holmes's profound disillusionment with the war as the stimulus for his move from transcendentalism to thoroughgoing skepticism.[37]

Surviving correspondence illuminates the context of crisis. By 1862 Holmes had become convinced that military victory was impossible.[38] He apparently first expressed his convictions in a letter to his sister at home, anticipating that she would bring his views to the attention of his father.[39] His father's predictable reaction—negative and judgmental—was forthcoming, and Holmes's response to his father resounded with anger and resentment. Addressing his father as "My Dear Governor," Holmes reasserted his conviction that victory was impossible, flaunted his greater knowledge and authority as a combatant, and accused his father of ignorance:

> It is in my disbelief in our success by arms in wh[ich] I differ from you. . . . I think in that matter I have better chances of judging than you—and I believe I represent the conviction of the army—& not the least of the most intelligent part of it. . . . I think you are hopeful because (excuse me) you are ignorant.[40]

Abundant evidence survives of Holmes's tensions with his father during the war.[41] He often addressed letters separately to his mother and father. Letters to his father about the military situation were

---

[37]Howe published two explanations of the crisis that differed in details. M. Howe, *The Positivism of Mr. Justice Holmes*, 64 *Harv. L. Rev.* 536–37 (1951); M. Howe, *supra* note 8, at 84, 109, 133, 136–38, 171–72.

[38]The view was widespread at the time and was supported by the apparent military impasse and decline in public enthusiasm. *See generally* L. Baker, *supra* note 4, at 137.

[39]Letter to his father, December 20, 1862, in O. Holmes, *Touched with Fire*, *supra* note 32, at 79—80.

[40]Letter of December 20, 1862 to his father, in *id.* at 79–80. *See* M. Howe, *supra* note 8, at 138.

[41]One episode entered folklore. In 1861, after Holmes's first wound, his father traveled to Philadelphia to meet him. M. Howe, *supra* note 4, at 101. After Holmes's near fatal wound in 1862, he wrote home, "I neither wish to meet any affectionate parent half way nor any shiny demonstrations when I reach the desired haven." Letter of September 22, 1862, in O. Holmes, *Touched with Fire*, *supra* note 32, at 67. Against his wishes his father traveled to meet him, recording the experience in a histrionic article published in *The Atlantic Monthly*. *See generally* L. Baker, *supra* note 4, at 133–36.

openly confrontational. Communicating his military despair in 1862, he attacked what he knew was one of his father's most cherished beliefs. The correspondence reveals deep hostility and confirms the collapse of the identification. A letter to "Dear Old Dad" in 1863 apologized for a "blow off" in the previous letter.[42] A letter in 1864 acknowledged receipt of recent letters, "the latter [letter] fr[om] dad, stupid."[43] Even the bloodletting of the war experience failed to restrain and channel his hostility.

The outbreak of conflict with his father during the war is enigmatic outside its emotional context.[44] In context the hostility emerges as unconscious motive for, rather than consequence of, views Holmes expressed to his father.

Holmes's father encouraged his entry into the war and later questioned his decision to leave the war. Holmes expressed particular outrage in a letter attacking the Boston news coverage of an encounter that had resulted in many unnecessary casualties: "I was glad to see that cheerful sheet [*Boston Daily Advertizer*] didn't regard the late attempt in the light of a reverse—It was an infamous butchery in a ridiculous attempt—in wh[ich] I've no doubt our loss doubled or tripled that of the Rebs."[45]

---

[42]Letter of March 29, 1863, in O. Holmes, *Touched with Fire*, *supra* note 32, at 86, 91. He apparently destroyed the previous letter.

[43]Letter of May 30, 1864, in *id.* at 135.

[44]Baker notes the sudden change in mood and explains it as the result of a sense of independence and maturity that Holmes acquired after leaving home and joining the army. L. Baker, *supra* note 4, at 142.

[45]Letter of December 20, 1862, O. Holmes, *Touched with Fire*, *supra* note 32, at 79. Later in the letter Holmes reminded his father that he remained "as ready as ever to do my duty." (*Id.* at 80). The theme of self-sacrifice and duty appeared repeatedly in his later writings. *E.g.*, O. Holmes, *Reflections on the Past and Future* (1912), in *The Occasional Speeches of Oliver Wendell Holmes* 167 (M. Howe comp. 1962).

The hostility that Holmes expressed toward his father during the war is consistent with a theory of a deep-seated infantile fantasy that his father wanted to kill him. But it may also simply reflect his anger at the decline and hypocrisy of enthusiasm for the federal war effort. Holmes's destruction of correspondence makes it impossible to establish the existence or effect of such a fantasy. Although I had previously suggested the existence of such a fantasy, Novick's speculative treatment of it has persuaded me that it is irresponsible to give any explanatory weight to the possibility of such a fantasy. *See* S. Novick, *supra* note 4, at 202, 446 n.43 ("apparently well-developed fantasy about the execution of unfit children . . . perhaps related to his own childlessness and his sense of having been sent by his parents to die in the Civil War."). *See also id.* 477–78 n.65 ("regular appearance in his writings of the theme of necessary sacrifice of children [no citations given], and the link he makes to the sacrifices made in war, suggest that Holmes

Conflict with his father continued and smoldered for years. In 1873, after visiting the Holmes home, Henry James wrote to his father: "[N]o love is lost between W[endell]. *pere* and W. *fils*."[46] In 1889 Holmes and his wife moved to his father's house, and Holmes complained, "My winter has not been sprightly, what with not feeling very well, and the adjustment to a new situation—living in my father's house instead in my own, etc."[47]

C. Allure of the Law

Holmes came close to death four times during the war. He suffered three gunshot wounds and contracted dysentery. His writings after the war make frequent reference to the war and are full of military imagery, yet he never talked of his personal experience in killing others. His decision to leave his regiment in 1864 when it was dissolved and merged into another was a difficult one, and one fraught with conflict with his father.[48]

While Holmes engaged in continuous conflict with his father during the war and tried literally to prevent his father from coming to him, Holmes returned home after each wound to maternal care—care that by replicating the mother-infant relationship connected trauma and pleasure and concealed and legitimized pleasure-seeking drives beneath Holmes's convalescent status. Most of his surviving war

---

unconsciously was repeating his parents' having sent him to war"). Except for the terrible language in the opinion in Buck v. Bell, 274 U.S. 200 (1927), Novick's argument is based largely on conjecture and tendentious interpretation of equivocal evidence.

[46]Letter of March 18, 1873, quoted in M. Howe, *supra* note 13, at 18.

[47]Letter of February 3, 1890, 1 Holmes-Pollock Letters, *supra* note 32, at 33. From the elder Holmes's letters, we know that Holmes's wife did much to brighten his father's last years and that Holmes was often out of the house. *See* 2 O. Holmes [Sr.], *supra* note 29, at 86–87, 263–64.

[48]The severity of Holmes's trauma, the compulsive intensity with which he withdrew into his work after the war, and the repeated use of military imagery in his later writings—all indicate the force of the trauma and are consistent with trauma-induced neurosis. Such a possibility raises limits to a theoretical explanation grounded on mental forces deriving from the oedipal complex. *See generally* S. Freud, *Beyond the Pleasure Principle*, 18 *The Standard Edition of the Complete Psychological Works of Sigmund Freud* 7–64 (J. Strachey trans. 1955). But his injuries alone do not increase the probability of such a neurosis. Freud observed that the concurrence of physical injury with psychic trauma actually reduced the likelihood of development of traumatic neurosis. *Id.* at 10.

letters were addressed to his mother. He wrote first to his mother with news of two of his three wounds and with news of his illnesses.[49]

Holmes may have been especially vigilant or successful in destroying correspondence that shed light on his relationship with his mother and his wife.[50] The record *seems* to indicate that he maintained a dispassionate intellectual relation with women. One Holmes biographer observed that "Holmes's friendships, whether with men or with women, were primarily intellectual."[51] Another wrote expansively of Holmes's self-imposed personal isolation.[52] But as Holmes destroyed much revealing documentation, appearances may be deceptive, and they conflict with important contemporary accounts.

Surviving letters reveal flirtatious relations with women. He addressed Lady Pollock "Beloved Lady" in response to a letter and wrote "I love seeing your dear handwriting again."[53] In 1910 he wrote to Lady Scott about reading sexual literature.[54] His flirtatious conduct toward a teenager during his first trip to England in 1866 led to some misunderstanding with her father.[55] During the Holmeses' trip to England in 1874 his flirting continued, and he teased his wife by signing an entry in her diary, "I sat next to Mrs. Willoughby whom I love."[56] She recorded later that week, "Wendell off on the rampage."[57]

From 1896 till 1926 Holmes engaged in an intimate correspondence with Lady Castletown in Ireland, whom he visited

---

[49]*See* O. Holmes, *Touched with Fire*, *supra* note 32, at 11, 13, 55, 56, 74, 92.

[50]He asked one writer to remove a reference to his wife in a published article. *See* letter to Elizabeth Shepley Sergeant, December 5, 1926, in The Oliver Wendell Holmes, Jr. Papers, *supra* note 7, reel 37. Holmes explained that his wife wanted no public attention.

[51]M. Howe, *supra* note 8, at 254. *See also* M. Howe, *supra* note 13, at 256–66.

[52]Rogat, *The Judge as Spectator*, 31 *U. Chi. L. Rev*. 227–28 (1964).

[53]Letter of January 10, 1904, 1 *Holmes-Pollock Letters*, *supra* note 32, at 115; letter of April 11, 1897, *id*. at 73.

[54]"I took up Casanova. . . . That was just what I wanted. . . . I don't like dirty books or care for indecent ones, but there sometimes goes with the freedom they imply, a temperament—a smack—a gusto, as I said, that puts life into one." Letter of May 27, 1910. Quoted in M. Howe, *supra* note 8, at 259.

[55]The misunderstanding is alluded to in a few letters relating to the episode that have survived. *See* M. Howe, *supra* note 8, at 231.

[56]The Oliver Wendell Holmes, Jr. Papers, reel 67. *See* M. Howe, *supra* note 8, at 99.

[57]*Id. See generally* L. Baker, *supra* note 4, at 234–35.

during trips to Europe in 1896, 1898, 1903, 1907, 1909, and 1913.[58] His wife's toleration for such flirting may have changed. According to contemporary rumors, his flirting deeply upset her, and she refused to read his letters from Europe until after his return for fear that he would describe his flirtatious conduct.[59]

Holmes's flirtatious behavior was notorious to contemporaries. Alice James, living in seclusion, wrote in her diary when Holmes returned to England in 1889, "They say he [Holmes] has entirely broken loose and is flirting as desperately as ever."[60] Later that year she recorded: "Henry says that Wendell Holmes has had a most brilliant success in London and that he was as pleasant as possible, young-looking, and handsomer than ever. Flirting as desperately too.—I suppose that his idea of 'Heaven is still flirting with pretty girls,' as he used to say."[61] Anecdotes about Holmes's flirting could be multiplied, and he continued to engage in such behavior in his later years.

His flirting was most often carried on during trips away from home with and without his wife, with married women and girls, with

---

[58]Holmes destroyed Lady Castletown's letters to him. Despite his request that she destroy his letters, at least 103 survived, and copies of them were donated to the Harvard Law School Library. The propriety of public treatment is moot. J. Monagan, "The Love Letters of Justice Holmes," *The Boston Globe Magazine* 15 (March 24, 1985); J. Monagan, *The Grand Panjandrum: Mellow Years of Justice Holmes* 71–94 (1988). It obviously cannot be proven that Holmes and his correspondent did *not* have a sexual affair—a possibility that preoccupies some of his biographers. But Holmes's literary intimacy with Lady Castletown is entirely consistent with his characteristic flirting, which did not result in sexual affairs and which, indeed, was motivated by his self-willed decision not to carry to completion the erotic drive disclosed by romantic behavior.

His relationship with Lady Castletown appears unique. The survival of evidence of the relationship was fortuitous, and the possibility that evidence of similar correspondence was destroyed cannot be eliminated. His letters to Lady Castletown express passion and intimacy, but the expressions of intimacy do not unambiguously suggest, let alone establish, anything further. Monagan interprets the letters as unequivocal evidence of an adulterous affair, but he neglects evidence to the contrary, such as the fact that Holmes wrote his correspondent's husband, "Please give her my love and tell her I think about her a great deal." Letter to Castletown, August 27, 1926, quoted in J. Monagan, *The Grand Panjandrum*, *supra* at 88.

[59]Mark DeWolfe Howe, typescript notes of interview with Mrs. James B. Ayer, October 25, 1955, The Oliver Wendell Holmes, Jr. Papers, *supra* note 50, reel 41.

[60]A. James, *supra* note 17, at 35.

[61]*Id.* at 61. Quotations *sic*, but *cf.* A. James, *Alice James: Her Brothers, Her Diary* 115 (A. Burr ed. 1934).

whom there was little risk of an actual sexual affair, and in correspondence at a safe distance. Even the exceptional outpouring of feeling in letters to Lady Castletown rarely rose to the ardent poetic expression of feeling in his postwar correspondence to William James: "Sing, sparrow—kissing with thy feet the topmost tassels of the pines."[62] Rather the flirting received safety from a self-controlled distance from women.[63] White observes, "In most of Holmes's letters his emotional feelings are unexpressed or tightly controlled."[64]

Detachment and distance in personal relations was especially pronounced in his relations with women. It surfaced paradoxically in flirting conduct that may, in a sense, have repeated early relationships with his mother. Distance certainly characterized his later relations with his mother. Writing of her death, Holmes communicated emotion but expressed distance by writing in the third person and adopting passive voice: "My mother's death was not to be regretted on her account but such an event whenever it happens must be a shock and give one a tug that goes far down to the roots."[65]

Holmes's "detachment" has come to be a cliche.[66] Holmes provided a clue to the defenses behind such distancing when he observed that [e]very man sees something of Mrs. Nickleby in his own mother."[67] The reference to the character of Mrs. Nickleby alluded to unresolved conflicting feelings toward his mother. The character of Mrs. Nickleby

---

[62]Letter to William James, April 19, 1868, in 1 R. Perry, *supra* note 3, at 511; *The Mind and Faith of Justice Holmes, supra* note 25, at 414. For a time Holmes struggled to find a more expressive salutation in his correspondence with Pollock, experimenting with "My Beloved Frederick" and "Dear F" before lapsing to "Dear Pollock," "My Dear Pollock" and, occasionally, Dear F.P." *See generally Holmes-Pollock Letters.*

[63]For a discussion of a different context in which distance increased the pleasure derived from an experience, *see* 2 P. Gay, *The Bourgeois Experience: Victoria to Freud* 392–93 (1984).

[64]White, *Holmes as Correspondent*, 43 *Vand. L. Rev.* 1707, 1734 (1990).

[65]Letter to Pollock, March 4, 1888, 1 *Holmes-Pollock Letters* 30. In reacting to his father's death in 1894, Aichele writes, "Holmes expressed solemnity rather than sorrow." G. Aichele, *supra* note 17, at 121.

[66]The term was ironically first used to describe his judicial personality by writers who, I believe, were unaware of the Casteltown letters and other evidence. But it is now a standard feature of Holmes biography. *See, e.g.*, L. Baker, *supra* note 4, at 157 ("detachment"); S. Novick, *supra* note 4, at 313 ("detachment"); G. Aichele, *supra* note 17, at x ("detachment").

[67]Alice James quoted this statement from memory. A. James, *supra* note 17, at 61. She recalled the statement in association with Holmes's statement about heaven being flirting with pretty girls and further recalled in association with these quotations: "which reminds me of Alice repeating Prof. Farlow's asking at their club table one night, 'why is every man's Aunt so entirely different from his Mother?'" *Id.*

was based on Dickens' own mother. The novel's plot further established the undercurrent of unresolved oedipal passions: after the death of the hero's father, the hero's mother witlessly sent the hero off to be mistreated at a boarding school, and witlessly assisted the attempted seduction of the hero's sister. The dramatic conflicts were resolved by the hero's marriage and by the violent death of the evil elder male characters.[68]

Psychoanalytic theory explains the conflict latent in Holmes's identification with his father and the hostility that he manifested toward his father as the expression of drives, with roots in his infancy and early childhood, for his mother's love. Legal scholarship after the war provided Holmes with new means for displacing erotic drives and for channeling and controlling aggression toward his father.

Legal scholarship and a legal career provided Holmes with methods for resolving deep conflicts, for creatively channeling powerful drives, for mastering the ego, and for constructing an identity for himself. In later years he came to associate his mature philosophical attitudes with his independence from his father. He emphasized that important features of his adult world view derived from his mother:

> My father was brought up scientifically . . . and I was not. Yet there was with him as with the rest of his generation a certain softness of attitude toward the interstitial miracle—the phenomenon without phenomenal antecedents, that I did not feel. . . . Probably a skeptical temperament that I got from my mother had something to do with my way of thinking.[69]

The accuracy of Holmes's autobiographical comments is uncertain. But the statement illustrates Holmes's desire to sever himself from his father's influence and to make real the fantasy—perhaps counterfactual—of his mother's intellectual influence.

---

[68]Mythic aspects of the plot and Mrs. Nickleby's character are discussed by H. Stone, *Dickens and the Invisible World: Fairy Tales, Fantasy, and Novel-Making* 82–85, 91 (1979). For a discussion of the author's use of his mother as prototype for Mrs. Nickleby and similar characters, *see* G. Watkins, *Dickens in Search of Himself: Recurrent Themes and Characters in the Work of Charles Dickens* 21–31 (1987).

[69]Letter of February 5, 1919, *The Holmes-Cohen Correspondence*, 9 *J. of the Hist. of Ideas* 14—15 (F. Cohen ed. 1948). *See also* The Oliver Wendell Holmes, Jr. Papers, *supra* note 50, reel 30 (typescript copy of letter). Baker reads "personal" for the second "phenomenal," which supports her inference that Holmes's father adhered to an anthropomorphic deism. L. Baker, *supra* note 4, at 67. *See also* manuscript letter to Fisher, November 3, 1897, The Huntington Library.

Holmes devoted extraordinary labor and emotional energy to legal study after the war. His preoccupation attracted the attention and concern of contemporaries. Before his 1866 trip to England his mother had counseled him by letter not to feel obliged "as you did at home that you must accomplish so much each 24 hours."[70] By the early 1870s Holmes was working on an ambitious new edition of Kent's *Commentaries on American Law*.[71] William James's mother described Holmes's obsession with the project, which was manifested by physical attachment to the manuscript:

> His whole life, soul and body, is utterly absorbed in his last work upon his Kent. He carries about his manuscript in his green bag and never loses sight of it for a moment. He started to go to Will's room to wash his hand, but came back for his bag, and when we went to dinner, Will said, "Don't you want to take your bag with you?" He said, "Yes, I always do so at home." His pallid face, and this fearful grip upon his work, makes him a melancholy sight.[72]

The emotional energy that Holmes brought to intellectual work after the war was focused with increasing intensity on law. William James noted with sadness the narrowing of Holmes's interests in 1868.[73] By 1872 James observed that Holmes "grows more and more concentrated upon his law. His mind resembles a stiff spring, which

[70]Letter to Holmes, quoted in part in M. Howe, *supra* note 8, at 280. *See also* letter of William James to Henry P. Bowditch, August 12, 1869, 1 W. James, *The Letters of William James*, 154–55 (H. James ed. 1920) ("I should think Wendell worked too hard"). John Ropes told William James that he never knew anyone who studied law as intensively as Holmes. Letter of William James to Bowditch, May 22, 1869, in 1 R. Perry, *supra* note 3, at 297. James wrote again in December that "Wendell Holmes is hard at work,—I fear too hard." Letter to Bowditch, *id.* at 321. In 1873 William James wrote his brother Henry, "I fear he [Holmes] is at last feeling the effects of his overwork." *Id.* at 337.

[71]J. Kent, *Commentaries on American Law* (12th ed. O. Holmes ed. 1873) (4 vols.).

[72]Quoted in 1 R. Perry, *supra* note 3, at 519. *See also* M. Howe, *supra* note 13, at 22. Holmes's wife told Mrs. Henry James that the publication of the work was a tremendous relief to "them." *Id.* The exchange between Mrs. Holmes and Mrs. James might appear to suggest that Mrs. Holmes was burdened emotionally by Holmes's scholarship, but in fact his wife played an active role in preparing the text for publication. *See* Little, *supra* note 11, at 186.

[73]Letter to Thomas W. Ward, December 16, 1868, 1 R. Perry, *supra* note 3, at 290 ("the sympathies we have in common are growing very narrowed").

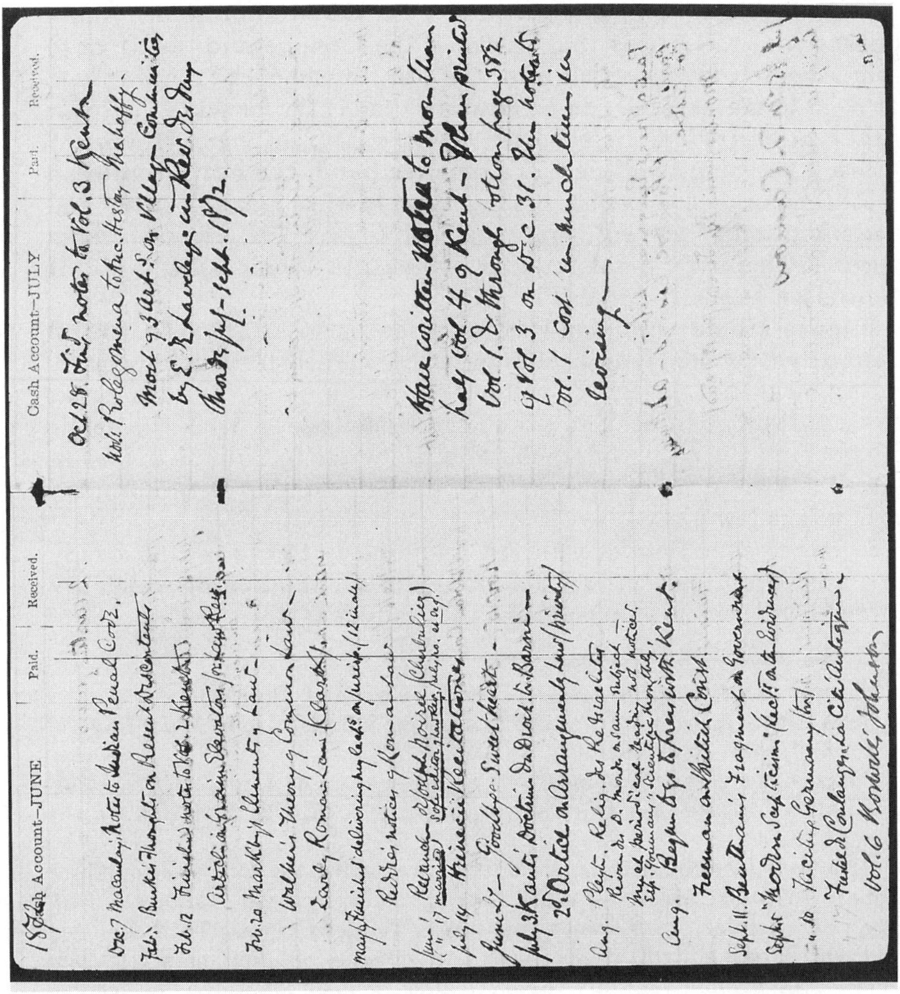

PLATE 7. Holmes's diary and reading list for Fall 1872. *Harvard Law School Library.*

has to be abducted violently from it, and which every instant it is left to itself flies tight back."[74]

Holmes carefully recorded the extraordinary range and intensity of his studies after the war.[75] He also left evidence in comments and unintentional references that revealed the force behind his drive to attain scholarly achievement after the war. In one of the reading lists that he kept methodically as an adult lies the entry for June 17, 1872: "[June] 17 *married*. Sole editor of Law Rev. July no. *et seq*."[76] Squeezed between two lines in a smaller hand, the entry conflated two contemporaneous events: his marriage to Miss Fanny Dixwell and his assumption of sole editorial responsibility for *The American Law Review*.[77] The entry amalgamated two events—achievements—that he unconsciously associated [Plate 7].

Intense scholarship was itself a defense, an attempt to control urgent drives by denial and sublimation.[78] But scholarship, especially reading, was not just a denial of reality; it gave Holmes great pleasure. Holmes himself toyed on a conscious level with the erotic drives behind the allure of scholarship. He wrote to William James in 1867: "For two or three months I debauched o'nights in philosophy. But now it is law—law—law."[79]

In later years Holmes referred humorously to the law as a lady and a mistress. He described the process of sublimation by which the allure of legal scholarship endowed the study of law with attributes of

---

[74]Letter to Henry James, November 24, 1872, in *id*. at 332.

[75]*See* Little, *supra* note 11, and The Oliver Wendell Holmes, Jr. Papers, *supra* note 7, reels 15 and 61.

[76]The Oliver Wendell Holmes, Jr. Papers, *supra* note 7, reel 16. *Cf*. Little, *supra* note 11, at 184. *See* L. Baker, *supra* note 4, at 222; S. Novick, *supra* note 4, at 133.

[77]He and co-editor Arthur G. Sedgwick replacing the *Review's* founding editors in 1870. *See* M. Howe, *supra* note 8, at 273; Kellogg, *Bibliographical Essay*, in O. Holmes, *The Formative Essays of Justice Holmes* 277 (F. Kellogg ed. 1984). Holmes edited the *American Law Review* from volume V (October 1870) through volume VII (July 1873). The *Review* itself identified neither the editors nor the authors of individual contributions. It is unclear whether Sedgwick withdrew as an editor in either 1872 or 1873. Howe writes that Holmes and Sedgwick turned over responsibility to the new editors, but he may have overlooked the diary entry. M. Howe, *supra* note 13, at 93–94.

[78]G. Blum, *Psychoanalytic Theories of Personality* 143–46 (1953). These defenses would typically arise in adolescence, and they were evident in Holmes's college writings, but their continuance and intensification after the war reflected his delayed and incomplete resolution of the resurgent oedipal complex. A. Freud, *The Ego and the Mechanism of Defense* 77–78 (C. Baines trans. 1946).

[79]Letter to William James, December 15, 1867, 1 R. Perry, *supra* note 3, at 505.

romantic attraction.[80] In one speech he eulogized law by extensive analogy: "If we are to speak of the law as our mistress, we who are here know that she is a mistress only to be wooed with sustained and lonely passion—only to be won by straining all the faculties by which man is likest to a god."[81] On another occasion he referred to students who serve "Truth, their only queen."[82] In comparing the lure of legal scholarship to romantic attraction, he deliberately played upon a theme that was familiar to his audience. Justice Story's famous speech upon taking the chair as Dane Professor of Law at Harvard in 1829 had referred to law: "It is a jealous mistress, and requires a long and constant courtship. It is not to be won by trifling favors, but by lavish homage."[83] By 1869 the phrase had become hackneyed.[84]

The assertion of the self in the midst of destructive forces was a theme to which Holmes returned many times in many contexts. He usually did not present it humorously but often invoked irony. His writings reveal fascination with military images, and he likened love and life generally to armed combat. It is not hard to find in this preoccupation echoes of his war experiences. The reassertion of life, self, and the pleasure principle in the face of reality naturally derived vital power from his own survival amidst despair. But the war was not the first source for such images. Holmes had used combat imagery in his college writings prior to any experience in combat. He had referred to Socrates as "a really great and humane spirit fighting the same fights with ourselves."[85] The poem from his senior year does not

---

[80]"I would not speak of Blackstone's 'superficial acquaintance' with the law. He was on pretty intimate terms with his lady." Letter to Wu, February 9, 1923, in *Justice Holmes to Dr. Wu: An Intimate Correspondence 1921–1923* 8 (J. Wu ed.[?] n.d.).

[81]*Speech at Suffolk Bar Association Dinner* (1885), in O. Holmes, *The Occasional Speeches*, *supra* note 45, at 21. He concluded: "But when for the first time I was called to speak on such an occasion at this, the only thought that could come into my mind, the only feeling that could fill my heart, the only words that could spring to my lips, were a hymm to her in whose name we are met here tonight—to our mistress, the Law." *Id.* at 23. *Cf.* Pollock's touching use of the analogy in a note to Holmes after Holmes's wife had died. 2 *Holmes-Pollock Letters*, *supra* note 32, at 245.

[82]*The Use of Law Schools: Oration Before the Harvard Law School Association* (1886), in O. Holmes, *The Occasional Speeches*, *supra* note 45, at 37.

[83]J. Story, *The Miscellaneous Writings of Joseph Story* 523 (W. Story ed. 1852).

[84]An 1860 memoir on Blackstone referred to the common use of the phrase. *See generally* Wigmore, *Diversities de la Ley*, 27 *Ill. L. Rev.* 329 (1933). *Cf.* R. Emerson, *The Conduct of Life* (1860), in *Ralph Waldo Emerson: Essays and Lectures* 1004 (J. Porte ed. 1983) ("Art is a jealous mistress").

[85]O. Holmes, *Plato*, 2 *The University Q.* 217 (1980).

survive, but a contemporary described its comparison of the graduating class to "a ship well-armed and equipped launched upon a wide sea."[86]

The intensity of Holmes's legal scholarship derived energy from powerful, infantile drives, but the direction and shape of scholarship were affected by the continuing hostile impulses toward his father. Holmes chose the law before the war. It was a scholarly discipline that his father had failed to master, and Holmes approached legal scholarship with a furious specialization that was foreign to his father. Holmes's articles published in the *American Law Review* in 1870–1873 were anonymous, technical studies in which he subordinated his views (and identity) to the authority of judicial precedent and emerging objective legal standards. Likewise, the extraordinary effort of Holmes in editing Kent's *Commentaries* required a powerful subordination of originality. The editorial work manifested values of painstaking, minute research and self-discipline in both effort and expression. Only the occasional footnote reveals the stunningly original views of Holmes on the evolution of liability.

Commitment to specialized study was reflected equally in Holmes's lectures and in *The Common Law* (1881). Extensive footnotes and discussion of cases purport to root all original generalizations in detailed study of legal developments. The preoccupation with specialization that is reflected in Holmes's scholarship was expressed also in his observations in later years to the effect that deep philosophical knowledge is approached by mastering the details of a narrow special area of study.

But one of Holmes's first defenses of specialization occurred in a letter to Emerson in 1876. Far from trying to distance himself from Emerson, the carefully composed letter acknowledged the influence of the great transcendentalist:

> I send by this mail the article of which I spoke. It is called "Primitive Notions in Modern Law." If the clothing of detail does not stand in the way I hope the ideas may not be uninteresting to you. It seems to me I have learned, after a laborious and somewhat painful period of probation that the law opens a way to philosophy as well as anything else, if pursued far enough, and I hope to prove it before I die. Accept this little piece as written in that faith, and as a slight mark of the gratitude and respect I feel for you who more than anyone else first started the philosophical ferment in my mind.[87]

---

[86] *Quoted in* M. Howe, *supra* note 8, at 75.

[87] The Oliver Wendell Holmes, Jr. Papers, *supra* note 50, reel 31, also *quoted in* M. Howe, *Justice Oliver Wendell Holmes, Jr.: Counsellor-At-Law* 8 (1948). He returned to this theme repeatedly. *See, e.g.*, Holmes, *Speech at*

In turning to the specialized study of law with such energy and emphasizing generally the value of specialization in scholarship, Holmes reacted against the work and style of his father. He later criticized his father's liberal scholarship and characterized it as something of a failure: "If he had the patience to concentrate all his energy on a single subject, which perhaps is saying if he had been a different man he would have been less popular, but he might have produced a great work."[88]

D. Identity and Originality

William James observed in 1869, "being ambitious of excellence he [Holmes] says the time is too short for the amount of work he is resolved to put into it, and it weighs heavy on his soul."[89] Holmes's biographers have noted Holmes's determination to achieve intellectual greatness.[90] Nearly a half century after the publication of *The Common Law*, he preserved the cork from the bottle with which he had celebrated the book's appearance and remembered how he had rushed to have it printed a few days before his birthday, "because then I should be 40 and it was said that if a man was to do anything he must do it before 40."[91]

The quest for intellectual recognition emerges as a powerful and conscious motive in Holmes's life, and it helps explain the broad contours of his intellectual biography after the war.[92] His quest for greatness, however, was only the conscious elaboration of emotional attitudes toward his own theories that had deep roots. The emotional depth of his feeling was expressed in a possessive attitude toward his work. "I can't help feeling in a personal way and wanting to beat the whole crowd—thinking about my work as *my* work and not simply as work which I hope may be useful."[93]

He was hostile and suspicious toward others who failed to attribute ideas to him that, he felt, derived from his work. In 1872 he

---

Brown Commencement (1897), in O. Holmes, *Collected Legal Papers* 166 (1921); 1 *Holmes-Pollock Letters*, *supra* note 32, at 16.

[88]Letter of July 26, 1914 to Clara Sherwood Stevens, *quoted in* M. Howe, *supra* note 8, at 19.

[89]Letter to Henry P. Bowditch, December 29, 1869, 1 R. Perry, *supra* note 3, at 321.

[90]*See generally* White, *supra* note 2, at 1409.

[91]Letter of October 12, 1930, to Mrs. Charles S. Hamlin, *quoted in* M. Howe, *supra* note 13, at 135.

[92]*See, e.g.*, *id.* at 10.

[93]Letter to Clara Sherwood Stevens of November 18, 1906, *quoted in* M. Howe, *supra* note 8, at 283.

sent a judge proofs of an article "The Theory of Torts." Holmes believed a decision by the judge was influenced by his article, but the decision did not acknowledge Holmes's work. For decades Holmes carried a grudge, and he recalled the experience in 1910 with bitterness. It affected his evaluation of the judge's work and character—"longwinded," "second rate discourses," "unfair," "not a great deal of brandy in his water."[94]

Even his friends did not escape his suspicion. He reproached Pollock, "I notice in the review . . . you speak of conflicting theories as to rebutting malice. . . . I put the matter in my book p. 139. You speak of Stephen having written on it—where has he done so? I had supposed that I started the point for the first time."[95]

Holmes's resentment contrasted sharply with his own failure to attribute ideas. This failure has bemused both theorists and biographers. Howe observes that *The Common Law* "borrowed from Maine,"[96] but Touster points out that the work does not acknowledge Maine.[97] Indeed, Holmes identified virtually no one as a significant influence on his intellectual development after college. Despite the close scholarship and authoritative attribution that he engaged in while editing *The American Law Review* and Kent's *Commentaries*, one searches in vain for citations that reveal sources of general theory or that disclose Holmes's extensive contemporaneous readings in philosophy or literature.

When Holmes was questioned directly about intellectual influence, he responded evasively. For example, though he read Spinoza's writings repeatedly, when Wu asked if Spinoza had influenced him, he denied that Spinoza had been a "conscious

---

[94]Letter of January 14, 1900, to Wigmore, *quoted in id.* at 84.

[95]Letter to Pollock of March 12, 1886, in *Holmes-Pollock Letters, supra* note 32, at 28. He had similarly complained to Thomas M. Cooley that Rufus Waples took ideas from *The Common Law* without attributing them to Holmes. *See* L. Baker, *supra* note 4, at 260.

[96]Howe, *Introduction,* in O. Holmes, *The Common Law* xiv (M. Howe ed. 1963). Howe's interpretation is questioned by H. Pohlman, *Justice Oliver Wendell Holmes and Utilitarian Jurisprudence* 2 (1984).

[97]"But Maine is conspicuous in *The Common Law* by his absence, suffering the additional indignity of having his thesis on the movement of the law from status to contract associated in a footnote with Blackstone!" Touster, *"Holmes's Common Law: a Centennial View,"* 51 *American Scholar* 527 (1982). Touster also observes, "Another great influence on Holmes, John Austin, is also neglected in *The Common Law.*" *Id.*

influence," conceding only that "the probability of an influence, even if indirect, is great."[98]

Caution about direct and indirect influence revealed insight into the complexity of influence. The failure to attribute important ideas manifested a fierce need for originality that had sources in drives of which he was not entirely aware. In 1919 Cohen asked Holmes about the influence of Voltaire on Holmes's skepticism, and Holmes responded: "Oh no—it was not Voltaire—it was the influence of the scientific way of looking at the world . . . I never have read much of Voltaire."[99] Denying reading "much" Voltaire is contradicted by his own meticulous records. They show he had read various works of Voltaire in 1877, 1883, and 1899.[100]

The denial appears to be the result of faulty memory, which is difficult to explain without the aid of psychoanalytic theory. Non-Freudian psychological models of memory generally stress that excited attention and repetition promote memory. But Holmes had read Voltaire repeatedly and had even read *Candide* and other works aloud in 1899. Voltaire's works are specially engaging, not easily forgotten.[101] Moreover, Holmes took real pride in the breadth of his readings, which he displayed in correspondence and listed. The denial revealed the power of Holmes's need for originality and novelty.

The impulses beneath Holmes's oblivion are illuminated by a similar experience that Freud recounted. In Freud's case, Freud proposed a theory to a colleague who reminded him that the colleague

---

[98]Letter of February 5, 1923, *Justice Holmes to Dr. Wu*, *supra* note 80, at 7–8; *Justice Oliver Wendell Holmes: His Book Notices and Uncollected Letters and Papers* 159 (H. Shriver ed. 1936).

[99]Letter of February 5, 1919, *Holmes-Cohen Correspondence*, *supra* note 69, at 14–15 (emphasis added).

[100]*See* Little, *supra* note 11, at 196; Black Book, Oliver Wendell Holmes, Jr., Papers, Harvard Law School Library, at 143 col. 1, at 155 col. 2.

[101]Memory loss is the most probable cause of the statement. I exclude the possibility of intentional misstatement. It is possible that Holmes meant only Voltaire's more technical works of philosophy. But Voltaire expressed his skeptical philosophy in his fiction as well as in his more didactic essays—indeed the distinction between literary and philosophical writings hardly applies to Voltaire's work.

Notwithstanding the memory lapse in 1919, Holmes wrote to Laski in 1924, referring to his having "glanced" at Voltaire's *Coquilles*. *See Holmes-Laski Letters* 580 1337 (M. Howe ed. 1953). In 1931 Holmes read two or three volumes of Voltaire's letters. Holmes, Black Book, *supra* note 100, at 71 col. 1. Although Holmes's need for originality led him to forget that he had repeatedly read Voltaire, it does not follow that Voltaire was an important influence. Holmes apparently read Voltaire after the development of his own skeptical world view. The episode demonstrates problems in relying on Holmes's autobiographical observations about his intellectual development.

had originally suggested the theory to Freud, but Freud had originally rejected the theory. Freud observed: "It is painful to be requested in this way to surrender one's originality. I could not recall any such [prior] conversation or this [prior] pronouncement of my friend's."[102] Only by reflecting on the dynamics of memory did Freud convince himself that he was mistaken. He subsequently recalled the original conversation.

Like Freud, Holmes forgot precisely in a context where questions of influence and originality were the subject of deliberate reflection. The pain of conceding nonoriginality for both thinkers effectively frustrated memory.

Denial of having read Voltaire is a clear and troubling example of Holmes's emphasis on novelty and his effort to free himself from the influence of earlier generations of thinkers. Denying the influence of Voltaire, he emphasized his youthful enthusiasm for Emerson and Ruskin. In his article *Natural Law* he forgot Emerson and Ruskin and wrote, "I use to say, when I was young, that truth was the majority vote of that nation that could lick all others."[103]

The relation of oblivion to unresolved hostility toward his father is further illuminated by the context of Holmes's explanation of his skepticism: he forgot reading Voltaire while emphasizing the gulf between his views and those of his father's generation.[104] And in forgetting intellectual antecedents, he traced the origins of his own skeptical temperament to his mother: "Probably a skeptical temperament that I got from my mother had something to do with my way of thinking."[105]

The deep roots of Holmes's continuing conflict with his father also help explain his conflicting memories of his father's role in his decision to enter law school. He recalled on one occasion that he was "kicked into the law by my governor [father]."[106] However, on the occasion of his ninetieth birthday, as Holmes savored the public

---

[102]S. Freud, *The Psychopathology of Everday Life,* in 6 *The Standard Edition of the Complete Psychological Works of Sigmund Freud* 144 (1960). *See also* Watson *Freud the Translator: Some Contacts with Philosophy,* 39 *The Int'l J. of Psycho-Analysis* 1–2 (1959) (discussing possible influences on Freud's theory of the pleasure, pain, and reality principles, which Freud forgot).

[103]O. Holmes, *Collected Legal Papers, supra* note 87, at 310.

[104]*Holmes-Cohen Correspondence, supra* note 69, at 15 n.27.

[105]*See id.* at 14. The close association of the memory of his mother's influence with the oblivion of Voltaire indicates the need for caution in assuming the accuracy of the memory, for the same dynamics that caused the oblivion could cause paramnesia.

[106]L. Baker, *supra* note 4, at 7 n.* (quoting Holmes's statement to Frankfurter in 1932).

celebration of his career, he could not help turning it into a victory over his father. He then recalled (perhaps erroneously) that his father had ridiculed and discouraged his interest in law school. Holmes remembered him asking, "What's the use of going to the Harvard Law School?"[107] And Holmes wished his father were alive again: "I wish that my father could have listened tonight for only two or three minutes. Then I could have thumbed my nose at him."[108]

E. Conflict in Legal Theory

Holmes worked to establish his intellectual identity as part of an ongoing struggle to control and master internal, conflicting drives. His struggle for control shaped the way he carved up his personal life into worlds of work and play.[109] Legal scholarship and judicial writing were themselves expressions of control—activities into which he directed all his energies.

His theory of law, too, reflected his central concern with conflict and control. He forged the philosophical perspective that supported his legal theory in opposition to the transcendentalism of his father. From an intellectual standpoint, "The clash between father and son may be regarded as symbolic of the impact on New England's transcendentalism of the positivism encouraged by the new theories of physics and biology."[110] From a psychoanalytic perspective, however, Holmes's effort to elaborate a science of law resulted from the clash with his father and from his internal struggle with the transcendentalism that he had assimilated through the process of identification.

The origins of the new theory do much to explain the emotional force with which it was expressed, and they illuminate Holmes's deep and abiding hostility to views that had once been his own. The natural law views associated with transcendentalism were special targets for his sarcasm and scorn—"fallacy and illusion,"[111] "irreconcilable with primary juridical notions."[112] He likened natural law to a child's bugaboo, "a brooding omnipresence."[113]

---

[107]*Id.* at 6 (*quoting* Holmes's statement to Laski in 1931).

[108]*Id.*

[109]White, *Holmes as Correspondent*, 43 *Vand. L. Rev.* 1707, 1757 (1990).

[110]P. Weiner, *Evolution and the Founders of Pragmatism* 173 (1969).

[111]Black & White Taxicab & Transfer Co. v. Brown & Yellow Taxicab Transfer Co., 276 U.S. 518, 533 (1928) (Holmes, J., dissenting).

[112]1 *Holmes-Pollock Letters*, *supra* note 32, at 39–40.

[113]Southern Pacific Co. v. Jensen, 244 U.S. 205, 222 (1917) (Holmes J. dissenting).

Holmes sought out conversations and correspondences with younger male intellectuals—sparring partners, toward whom he adopted antagonistic intellectual postures that continue to bewilder biographers.[114] In these relationships Holmes replicated his relation with his father; he avoided confronting his chronological or social superiors and assumed an antagonistic paternal relation with his inferiors. The relationships demonstrated the extraordinary plasticity of Holmes's superego, and the lengths to which he would go to cultivate intellectual pugilism. According to one account, Holmes challenged his conversational adversary, "I am ready to contradict any statement you will make."[115]

Holmes rejected vehemently all utopian schemes premised on the elimination of tension. Though he expressed conviction infrequently after the 1860s, he expressed forcefully his rejection of utopian ideologies that assumed the eventual elimination of social conflict. "Of course I disbelieve in all utopias to be reached through *property*."[116] He reacted cynically to Franklin Ford's optimistic view of the future development of society on "the basis of science."[117] His frequent jibes at pacifism are well known, and he characterized egalitarian economic theories as "drivelling cant."[118]

A central feature of Holmes's thought was recognition and acceptance of tension. In *The Path of the Law* (1897), he wrote:

---

[114]*See, e.g., Progressive Masks: Letters of Oliver Wendell Holmes, Jr. and Franklin Ford* 17 (D. Burton ed. 1982). He corresponded extensively with Sheehan, Laski, Pollock, Wu, Ford, and Einstein. Only Pollock was his contemporary and only Pollock had comparable social standing. Holmes was born in 1841, Pollock in 1845, Ford in 1849, Sheehan in 1852, Einstein in 1877, Laski in 1893, and Wu in 1899.

[115]The widow of Glendower Evans recalled this statement from hearsay many years later. It is quoted in L. Baker, *supra* note 4, at 245; *see also* S. Novick, *supra* note 4, at 165. Baker and Novick quote the source as fact, but reasons for questioning the literal accuracy of this kind of statement are self-evident from its attribution and date.

[116]Letter of June 18, 1911 to Alice Green, The Oliver Wendell Holmes, Jr. Papers, *supra* note 50, reel 32. Holmes characterized socialist theories as "drool." 1 *Holmes-Laski Letters, supra* note 101, at 96.

[117]*Progressive Masks, supra* note 114, at 109.

[118]Letter to Wu of June 21, 1928, *Justice Holmes to Dr. Wu, supra* note 80, at 48; and in O. Holmes, *Justice Oliver Wendell Holmes: His Book Notice and Uncollected Letters and Papers, supra* note 98, at 197.

> If you want to know the law and nothing else, you must look at it as a bad man, who cares only for the material consequences which such knowledge enables him to predict, not as a good one, who finds his reasons for conduct . . . in the vaguer sanctions of conscience.[119]

His theory of criminal law explained criminal prohibitions as social efforts to deter unwanted acts, and he neglected considerations of moral blame-worthiness.[120] After his death his focus on the bad man and his treatment of criminal law came under attack.[121]

Holmes's approach to criminal law and his use of the "bad man" thought experiment in the *Path of the Law* were not just formal approaches that exalted prediction. They expressed an attitude toward human motivation that incorporated the view that, as Freud put it, "[A]s regards conscience God has done an uneven and careless piece of work, for a large majority of men have brought along with them only a modest amount of it or scarcely enough to be worth mentioning."[122]

Recognizing real limits to the efficacy of legal control in theory, Holmes expressed the sense of his own limits and powerlessness. Thus the struggle for control and concomitant appreciation of limits shaped his life as it did his theory. "Powerlessness and power-seeking thus became the final, and perhaps the organizing, themes of Holmes's life plan."[123]

Rejecting the transcendentalist dream of a lawless world of good men,[124] Holmes recognized implicitly the permanent inner conflict of forces, held in check only by an internal constabulary and supported by its external counterpart. Acceptance and control of conflict informed his mature political values and characterized the legal and constitutional positions for which he is best known, from toleration of labor organization to defense of free speech to deference to social welfare legislation.

---

[119]O. Holmes, *Collected Legal Papers, supra* note 87, at 171.

[120]O. Holmes, *The Common Law* 39–76 (1881).

[121]*See, e.g.*, L. Fuller, *The Law in Quest of Itself* 93 (1940); Allen, *Criminal Law*, 31 *U. Chi. L. Rev.* 257 (1964); Atiyah, *The Legacy of Holmes through English Eyes*, in Kaplan, Atiyah, and Vetter, *Holmes and the Common Law: A Century Later* 29–36 (Holmes Devise Lectures 1983); Rogat, *supra* note 52, at 213–24.

[122]S. Freud, *New Introductory Lectures on Psycho–Analysis* (1933), 22 *The Standard Edition of the Complete Psychological Works of Sigmund Freud* 61 (1964).

[123]White, *supra* note 2, at 1474.

[124]*See* R. Emerson, *Essays: Second Series*, in *Ralph Waldo Emerson: Essays and Lectures* 566–69 (1983).

Internalization and reproduction of conflict also provided the mechanics for his theory of legal history. Holmes saw legal history as a process of evolutionary growth, shaped by external social conflict, by internal conflict of competing ideas, and by the mediating force of law in structuring society. Law developed through a constant process analogous to natural selection and adaptation.[125] Law developed progressively, but the goal of history was not elimination of conflict, for law progressed only in response to the constant tension between old and new, anachronism and legislation, in the present.[126]

His goal in law and in legal theory was to make the process explicit to understanding: "Hitherto this process has been largely unconscious. It is important, on that account, to bring to mind what the actual course of events has been."[127] By making law and legal history self-aware, Holmes expanded the scope of freedom. But freedom resulted from the creative channeling of previously unconscious drives and conflicts, not by abolishing them.[128]

In the end, Holmes failed to live up to Jerome Frank's myth. His life was more complicated, and his thought was more interesting. Holmes neither destroyed the authoritative claims of law nor did he ultimately construct a consistent view of the world in which law operated instrumentally as means to some end. In law understood as historical process, authority resulted from pervasive and permanent conflict, not resolution. His theories sought to elaborate the grounds of the conflict and to explain legal historical change as a progressive response to and repetition of the conflict.

---

[125]Holmes's evolutionary treatment of legal process is discussed by Wiener, *Evolution and the Founders of Pragmatism, supra* note 110, at 175–82, and Elliott, *Holmes and Evolution: Legal Process as Artificial Intelligence,* 13 *J. Legal Studies* 113, 114–43 (1984).

[126]*See, e.g., O. Holmes, The Common Law, supra* note 120, at 35. His appreciation of the quantity of change over time itself changed in later years, but the basic operative mechanics remained constant. For a discussion of Holmes's theory of change and his changing attitude toward the rate of change, *see* Elliott, *supra* note 125, at 135–36.

Baker expresses a common view when she writes, "That the law's development might have been progressive was not generally recognized," L. Baker, *supra* note 4, at 249. *See also id.* at 257 ("Blackstone's theory that the law, given by God Himself, was immutable and eternal."). But Holmes's historicism was not new. The transcendentalists embraced a progressive historical vision of history, and Justice Story defended a developmental theory of common law.

[127]O. Holmes, *The Common Law, supra* note 120, at 36.

[128]Holmes's attitudes toward American political and legal history confirm this. *See* J. Hurst, *Justice Holmes on Legal History* 123–29 (1964).

Epilogue

TWO GENERATIONS ago, John Wu observed that Holmes's philosophy of law incorporated powerful idealist elements. Wu maintained his interpretation over the years and later wrote that "it is not easy to say whether Holmes is an idealist or a positivist. He is both, just as the common law is a combination of the actual and the ideal."[1] Preoccupation with instrumental features of Holmes's thought led to neglect of Wu's insight. But even before Wu, Holmes acknowledged that he was reputed to be something of a mystic. He did not reject the characterization and observed "we are all mystics at bottom, for we recognize that the universe contains all we know and more—and what that more is is mystery."[2]

Holmes saw legal theory as an entry into philosophy. In part, this reflected his opinion that all specialized study could lead to broader philosophical truth, that "one part of the universe yields the same teaching as any other if only it is mastered."[3] Holmes also seemed to ascribe a special status to legal scholarship that reflected law's unique combination of theory and practice. He saw himself as a philosopher, even in his legal work, not just a technician or a predictor. His most important theoretical effort, *The Common Law*, seemed far removed from transcendentalism in its approach and style. Nevertheless, the book reflected the influence of transcendentalist attitudes in its general goal and in its organization and treatment of particular legal topics.

The narrator's goal in the work was to raise the awareness of the process of legal development to self-consciousness. This was positivist only in the trivial sense that Holmes recognized that a developmental factor was the unarticulated policies behind legal rules. It was pragmatic only in the sense that it tended to legitimate more direct recourse to policy as a ground of decision. Its central purpose,

[1]Wu, *Justice Holmes and the Common Law Tradition*, 14 *Vand. L. Rev.* 221, 226 (1960). *See* Wu, *The Juristic Philosophy of Justice Holmes*, 21 *Mich. L. Rev.* 523 (1923).

[2]Letter of December 27, 1913, to Alice Green, The Oliver Wendell Holmes, Jr. Papers (University Publications of America, 1985) (Microfilm Project), reel 32.

[3]*Speech at Brown Commencement*, in O. Holmes, *Collected Legal Papers* 166 (1921).

however, was not further justified. Raising consciousness to self-awareness—the pursuit of theoretical understanding for its own sake—incorporated one of the ideals of the transcendentalists. The process of self-awareness was not defined in terms of enhanced functional effectiveness of legal prediction but rather in terms of human freedom.[4]

Holmes's selection of legal topics in *The Common Law* revealed his commitment to a search for the generalizing and cohesive aspects of law that were associated with traditional natural law doctrine. The goal shaped his organization of material in the book and explains important omissions. Thus he omitted a separate treatment of agency law—an important topical area in the nineteenth century and a subject that he had taught—because agency provided no obligations and correlative rights; agency only explained the transfer of such obligations and rights by means of the fiction of identity of principal and agent.[5] *The Common Law* was preoccupied with the rational evolution of a unified theory of liability. In a later marginal note that Holmes made to his own copy of the book he wrote, "I propose to show that the true bond of union of all these [early forms of liability] is not to be found in the various grounds of policy wh[ich] have been mentioned but in one wh[ich] is com[mon] to them all."[6]

Holmes's legal theory transformed natural law in two crucial ways. First, Holmes rejected the accessibility of natural law to the individual and transformed it into something that manifested itself only to groups—above all, to self-aware groups. Second, he rejected the notion that natural law existed before or independent of its social

---

[4]*See* Holmes, *Law in Science and Science in Law*, in O. Holmes, *Collected Legal Papers*, *supra* note 3, at 225 ("History sets us free . . ."). Kelley argues for a positivist influence from the general three-part developmental scheme that he finds revealed in the progressive history in *The Common Law*. *See* Kelley, Book Review, 68 *Wash. U.L.Q.* 429,452 (1990). But his exposition of the book's developmental scheme does not show how it was radically different from progressive developmental schemes of idealist and transcendental philosophers current before Comte.

[5]The omission of agency certainly did not reflect his opinion that the subject was legally unimportant, though his treatment no doubt played an important part in the contemporary lack of interest in the subject. Holmes did not think agency was unimportant, nor did he avoid it because it did not illustrate points that he sought to make in the book. In fact, he had previously treated agency law at some length, and his history of agency provided important examples of the dynamics of legal development that he proposed. His study of agency law may even have helped stimulate the general historical theory advanced in *The Common Law*, and he later republished his work on agency. Holmes, *Agency*, in *Collected Legal Papers*, *supra* note 3, at 49–116.

[6]O. Holmes, *The Common Law* 9 n.d. (Howe ed. 1963).

manifestation; he transformed it into something that emerged only over time. Nevertheless, in replacing an absolute concept of law with an evolutionary and historical one, Holmes adopted transcendental standards—standards against which the actual law at any time was measured. Good law was increasingly objective and concrete. Good legal theory produced ever more objective and concrete law by making the grounds of law explicit and by making law comport with its grounds. Holmes labored to develop a general theory to explain the apparent diversity of cases and rules.[7]

Holmes's skepticism incorporated lessons he learned from his conflict with his father during the Civil War. His skepticism revealed his rejection of the certainty of individual knowledge; but he did not cynically reject the values of either the individual or group. On the contrary, Holmes looked to the outcome of historical development to validate the claims of such values.[8]

Despite his tough Malthusian realism, and notwithstanding recurrent bouts of depression, Holmes embraced an abiding optimism in process and group development. "[W]hen Harvard College is no longer dedicated to truth and America to democratic freedom; then, perhaps, but not till then, will the blood of the martyrs be swallowed in the sand and the Puritan have lived in vain."[9] His optimism was arguably also his greatest weakness as a judge and source of some of his most troubling opinions. An underlying faith in his country and its institutions helps account for the ease with which he deferred to legislation. Critics interpreted his views as a defense of state power—"might makes right." But his optimism provided the firm ground that supported such remarks: he was confident at bottom that the long-term development of the group did in fact promote right. This tacit appeal to the future also expressed a basic attitude traditionally associated with transcendental natural law theory.

Holmes's optimism must be understood in historical context. His celebration of the power of law and his deference to legislation reflected faith in progressive democratic process that was sustained by the surprising outcome of the Civil War and by the course of

---

[7]*See* G. White, *Tort Law in America: An Intellectual History* 13–19 (1985).

[8]*See* Elliott, *Holmes and Evolution: Legal Process as Artificial Intelligence*, 13 *J. Legal Studies* 113, 139 (1984) (describing Holmes's view of law as a "system" of evolving intelligence in which "[t]he law may hope to be wiser than the individuals who make it").

[9]Address of February 7, 1886, at the services commemorating the 250th anniversary of First Church, Cambridge. Program at 90, in The Oliver Wendell Holmes, Jr. Papers, *supra* note 2, reel 65. *See also* O. Holmes, *The Occasional Speeches of Justice Oliver Wendell Holmes* 25–26 (M. Howe comp. 1962).

American civilization for most of his life. It was certainly inaccurate to read Holmes as a personal friend of social reform, as liberal followers were wont to do. It is no less inaccurate to read Holmes as a cynical proponent of state force for its own sake, as critics have done.[10] The central tension—rooted deeply in his emotional and biographical development and manifested in his philosophical, political, and historical views—cannot be eliminated.

Appreciating the way Holmes transformed natural law illuminates a critical period in American cultural and political history—the convergence of ideology and the compromise of conflicting commitments in the generation after the Civil War. Holmes's intellectual development curiously paralleled that of his nemesis, Justice L.Q.C. Lamar, antediluvian partisan of natural law and author of the only opinion that ever reversed Holmes.

On the surface Holmes and Lamar were polar opposites in every way. Before the Civil War they took opposite and absolute positions on the slavery question.[11] Yet after the war Holmes and Lamar participated in the reunification of the country. Meador singles out Lamar's appointment to the Supreme Court as "the last step toward national reconciliation and reunion in the long aftermath of the Civil War."[12]

Holmes and Lamar differed on fundamentals of legal theory, and Holmes protested against Lamar's natural law reasoning in the opinion reversing him. Nevertheless, the apparent opposition of the two should not obscure the fact that the ideology of both underwent an important transformation after the Civil War that resulted in a convergence. Lamar's transformation was public: his eulogy of Sumner in 1874 became one the great events of the day. Its closing

---

[10]Critics, beginning in the 1940s, changed radically their grounds of criticism. In doing so they failed to appreciate the extent to which they were themselves reacting to different historical perceptions and failed to appreciate that Holmes (for example, in deferring to state authority) manifested optimism not totalitarianism. Contrast the different attitudes toward militarism expressed by critics of Holmes's rejection of natural law in Zane, *German Legal Philosophy*, 16 *Mich. L. Rev.* 345–46 (1918); Zane, *A Legal Heresy*, 13 *Ill. L. Rev.* 255 (1918), and *L. Fuller, the Law in Quest of Itself* 106–07 (1940).

[11]*See* D. Boorstin, *Hidden History* 159–75 (1987) (discussion of common appeal of conflicting traditions to unwritten law).

[12]D. Meador, *Lamar to the Court: Last Step to National Reunion, Supreme Court HIstorical Society Yearbook* 1986 22, 27 (1986).

lines electrified the nation: "My countrymen! *Know* one another, and you will *love* one another."[13]

Holmes's transformation occurred in private and resulted in extraordinary, original works of legal scholarship. In the end, however, both Holmes and Lamar advanced arguments that supported consensus but did not require individuals to agree on important conflicting moral values. Lamar's eulogy "carefully praised Sumner as a man utterly dedicated to individual liberty, but at the same time avoided any indication that the South had been wrong on the [slavery] question."[14] Holmes, too, adopted rhetorical techniques that sought to win consent and establish community by inviting persons with conflicting values to seek unity in higher values. Lamar appealed to mutual understanding and love. Holmes, too, employed the rhetoric of transcendence to resolve—and evade—the most difficult and divisive issues.[15]

Within the legal community, convergence and consensus were effected by increasing reliance on procedural, morally neutral policy arguments. Many of the general trends of law in this century—the expansion of federal jurisdiction (power) simultaneously with a relinquishing of efforts to ground that power in claims of substantive law, the decline of substantive due process, the Erie doctrine, the elaboration of procedural standards of review in criminal law and administrative proceedings—witness the continuation of trends that Holmes and Lamar helped initiate.

Holmes and Lamar came to recognize in the period after the Civil War that transcendental claims could no longer be advanced by the individual without challenge—that indeed such claims could be disruptive of the community. Both placed greater value on abstract values that provided the basis for consensus but challenged the moral

---

[13]*Quoted in* E. Mayes, *Lucius Q.C. Lamar: His Life, Times, and Speeches 1825–1893* 184–87 (1896); W. Cate, *Lucius Q.C. Lamar: Secession and Reunion* 4 (1935).

[14]J. Murphy, *L.Q.C. Lamar: Pragmatic Patriot* 116 (1973).

[15]Dudziak argues that "it was through the power of his literary form that Holmes most clearly expressed the opinions that, in his view, were most appropriately held to himself." Dudziak, *Oliver Wendell Holmes as a Eugenic Reformer: Rhetoric in the Writing of Constitutional Law*, 71 *Iowa L. Rev.* 833, 866 (1986). Schwartz interprets *The Path of the Law* as resting on a scheme that proceeds from a statement of contradiction to rhetoric of transcendence: "Apparently recognizing that dialectic always espouses contraries, Holmes employs the rhetorical strategy of transcendence so as to rise above the actual contraries within the law and instead moves into the realm of potentiality for law where everyone can agree." Schwartz, *Oliver Wendell Holmes's "The Path of the Law": Conflicting Views of the Legal World*, 29 *Am. J. Legal Hist.* 235, 249 (1985).

commitment of neither North nor South. The negative features of the post-Civil War consensus are clear in hindsight—the apology for the status quo, the abandonment of interests of blacks. Positive features of the abstract values embedded in Holmes's and Lamar's language of transcendence included tolerance, resignation, and willingness to wait and abide by the outcomes of historical processes that remained unknowable to the individual.

APPENDIX A

The Early Critical and Philosophical Writings

HOLMES'S college writings were published in the following order:

Books	*The Harvard Magazine*, vol. 4, 408–12 (December 1858)
Editors' Table	*The Harvard Magazine*, vol. 7, 26–27 (September 1860)
Editors' Table	*The Harvard Magazine*, vol. 7, 37–38 (September 1860)
Notes on Albert Durer	*The Harvard Magazine*, vol. 7, 41–47 (October 1860)
Alma Mater	*The Harvard Magazine*, vol. 7, 48 (October 1860)
Plato	*The University Quarterly*, vol. 2, no.4, 205–17 (October 1860)
Book Notices	*The Harvard Magazine*, vol. 7, 11–12 (November 1860)
Book Notices	*The Harvard Magazine*, vol. 7, 235–36 (March 1861)
Pre-Raphaelitism	*The Harvard Magazine*, vol. 7, 345–48 (June 1861)

Holmes published *Books* in his sophomore year. At the end of his junior year (July 1860) he became co-editor of *The Harvard Magazine* for his class along with Albert Stetson and Wendell Phillips Garrison (son of abolitionist William Lloyd Garrison).[1]

During the summer vacation in 1860 he wrote *Plato* and *Notes on Albert Durer*.[2] *Plato* appeared that fall in *The University Quarterly*, an intercollegiate publication that had been founded the previous year; the article received the prize for the best undergraduate contribution for 1860.[3] *Notes of Albert Durer* and the poem *Alma*

[1]*See* L. Baker, *The Justice From Beacon Hill: The Life and Times of Oliver Wendell Holmes 87* (1991); M. Howe, *Justice Oliver Wendell Holmes: The Shaping Years 1841–1870* 293 n.45 (1975).

[2]*See infra*, notes 11 and 23.

[3]*See* M. Howe, *supra* note 1, at 60 & 293 n.48.

Mater appeared about the same time as *Plato*. Holmes also authored four or five[4] short editorial pieces that were published during his senior year—a short descriptive review of three titles, a scathing review of a parlor romance, and two editorial communications. The four short articles were less ambitious than his sophomore publications. Motivated in part by editorial duties,[5] he may not have considered them important, and he did not include them in his volume of college essays.

Holmes's last prewar article, *Pre-Raphaelitism*, appeared in print after Holmes had joined the Massachusetts regiment. A "Program of the Order of Performances for Exhibition on May 7, 1861" recorded that Holmes was schedules to have delivered "A Disquisition on Pre-Raphaelitism," but Holmes never gave the speech because he had entered military service.[6] The article may have been the text that he had prepared for delivery during his senior year.[7] It, too, was omitted from his collection of college publications.[8]

The texts published here follow the originals and preserve the original spelling and punctuation. Handwritten notes and corrections

---

[4]The typescript index to volumes one through ten of *The Harvard Magazine* at Harvard University Archives attributes the review of *Autobiography of the Rev. Alexander Carlyle*, 7 *Harvard Magazine* 230–32 (1861), to both Holmes and Garrison. The archives' issue of the *Magazine* also has a tentative attribution of the work in pencil: "Holmes?" But the Hackett index did not attribute the review to Holmes, and Howe ignored it. The protemperance views and treatment of religion in the review suggest that Garrison was the author. *Compare* Holmes, *Editor's Table*, 7 *Harvard Magazine*, at 37. But it cannot be ruled out that Holmes entertained such views in college or that he collaborated with Garrison in writing the review. The review's interest in the engraved portrait comports with Holmes's interests.

[5]The last paragraph of the *Editors' Table*, 7 *Harvard Magazine*, at 26–27, indicates that the *Magazine* had difficulty obtaining good submissions. The anonymous essays are attributed to Holmes by the indices at Harvard University Archives.

[6]The program is preserved, O. Holmes Papers, Harvard Law School Library. *See College Record*, 7 *Harvard Magazine*, June 1861, at 357 (noting that Holmes's disquisition was "omitted").

[7]*See* M. Howe, *supra* note 1, at 60.

[8]Holmes also did not preserve a copy of the poem he delivered at Class Day in 1861. *See* M. Howe, *supra* note 1, at 75–76. The absence of the poem and the article on Pre-Raphaelitism might be explained by his move to camp during his senior year. The only work referred to in his *Autobiographical Sketch* was *Notes of Albert Durer*.

that Holmes made on his copies of *Books*, *Notes on Albert Durer*, *Alma Mater*, and *Plato* are included in footnotes.[9]

A. Holmes's College Publications

1. Books[10]

The highest conversation is the statement of conclusions, or of such facts as enable us to arrive at conclusions, on the great questions of right and wrong, and on the relations of man to God. And so we all know well enough the difference, in our various associates, between him who lives only in events, and can relish nothing but the College gossip for the day, and him who feels that this is well enough, but that he can find higher food for thought, and who, while still young, passes restless hours longing to find some one who will talk to him of better things. Those, then, who have somewhat higher aspirations than the mass of their companions, and who in the ranks of boyish insipidity find none who meet or satisfy their desires, must as an alternative take to books.

And, again, many even of the somewhat unthinking will resolve every day to "read," (a phrase of slightly indefinite meaning, even to those who use it,) but, every day discouraged by the enormous quantity of books pronounced "indispensable," end by reading nothing. But this is very unnecessary trouble. Books are now almost innumerable, and most of them have been written within three hundred years. Regarding, then, what has been done already by mighty minds, and looking forward on the futurity we may reasonably suppose to be still remaining for this world, we see that the time is not inconceivably distant when a bookworm's life shall be spent in perusing a literature of Shakespeares and Prophets. This view, it is evident, will very materially contract the importance to be attached to any single volume, and will show two or three rules to be all that can be laid down with any real certainty.

---

[9]I rely on Howe's identification of the handwriting. *See* M. Howe, *supra* note 1, at 54 n.d; Holmes, Uncollected Essays and Reviews 1858–1870 (Howe ed. unpublished typescript) (Holmes Papers, Harvard Law School Library). Marginal notes were in pencil, and Holmes probably made some of the marginal notes soon after publication, but the orthography suggests that notes were made at different times.

[10]The copy of the article that Holmes collected with his other early essays was originally presented to his father. At its head is the presentation in pen: "O W. Holmes/ from the Author—O.W.H. Jr."

First, then, we must read for ideas, not for authors. And we shall find that every grand book carries with it and implies ten thousand lesser ones; just as, when a huge tree is torn from the ground, it carries along with its roots an entire body of weeds and flowers and saplings. We read the Bible, and do not feel the need of Doctor Johnson's instructions in morality; and after studying the works of William Shakespeare, we find that Addison's Cato can teach us nothing. The first two contain all the last, and a great deal to spare; as I said in the beginning, they imply them.

Secondly, I cannot get beyond the belief that it is best to read what we like; there must be some book or books not absolutely vicious which would be interesting to any reader of this Magazine, and these, whatever they be, will necessitate a certain degree of thought, which of itself is sufficient cause for a better choice in the second instance. Of course a certain number selecting simply by preference would choose certain yellow-clad volumes and newspapers not of the best; but they are capable of higher things, and the rule is good. A great reader said, "As soon as you forget the color of the heroine's hair, lay down the book." We must read no longer—of course I speak of such reading as fills the intervals of other study, and does not itself form our labor—we must read no longer than we are perfectly engrossed in our subject.

Thirdly, for the description of books. After what has been said, it is sufficiently evident that but few rules can be laid down when we start by leaving all to individual judgment; but this may be suggested. First, as for the great books of other tongues, there are in each language one, or perhaps two or three geniuses, that have, as it were, originated the very literature of that state and period from which they sprung; that, like the loadstone mountain of the Arabian Nights, have drawn to their own mighty bulk the nails and strength of the time, and, while everything around them has fallen to pieces, stand only in increased power and majesty. These we must know; but for the Antoninuses and Thomas a Kempises, the reflectors and commentators, their spirit is the same in one language as in another, our native English furnishes enough of them, and, moreover, all the fine ideas that were their *end* are in the books of the present day the assumed axioms from which we start. But more important than all this, we must at once in some shape understand the questions of the day. Just as one man implies humanity, so the history of the struggles of one period implies eternity. And though there always is a fight and crisis, yet are we not in a peculiarly solemn position? Books and papers, within a century or two only accessible to the common people, have had their effect. A hundred years ago we burnt men's bodies for not agreeing with our religious tenets; we still burn their souls. And now some begin to say, Why is this so? Is it true that such ideas as this come from God? Do men own other men by God's law? And when these questions are asked around us,—when we, almost the first of young men who have been brought up in an atmosphere of investigation, instead of having every doubt answered, It is written,—when we begin to enter the fight, can we help feeling it is a tragedy? Can we help going to our rooms and crying that we might now think? And we whistle or beat on our piano, and some—God help 'em!—smoke and drink to drive it all away, and others find their resting-place in some creed which defines all their possibilities, and says, Thus far shall ye think, and no farther. No, no; it will not do to say, I am not of a melancholic temperament, and mean to have any good time. It will not do for Ruskin to say, Read no books of an agitating tendency; you will have enough by and by to distress you. We *must*, will we or no, have every train of thought brought before us while we are young, and may as well at once prepare for it.

History should be the finest, in fact, the all-comprehending study. But we do not find it so. The cause, as it seems to me, being that facts and dates are mistakenly supposed to constitute its chief part. Yet, if we think, we shall know that these are not what impress us with the realities of past time. Little things—anecdotes—will often display the whole manners and customs of a period, when we should have laid down the statistics as ignorant as we took them up. What is most pleasant about Herodotus is, that, in a history of the great nations of the earth, he tells us such facts as that the mares that gained three races are buried by the side of their master in the road that runs through the Hollow. This history, which we can by no possibility get, except by fragments from contemporary plays and poems, with regard to past days, at present we can have, or almost have forced upon us by the daily newspapers, reading in them details about each day enough to fill a volume of Grote or Macaulay. And so I say again, we must study the present to know the past. Emerson, who probably takes about as large a view of men and events as any one we could point out now living in America, gains much of this breadth by the peculiar direction of his studies. Look into his article on Books,—never was a stranger list of indispensables, will be our first impression. But we shall soon see the plan that regulates him. *We* read principally, more even than we do Shakespeare or any great man who lived as many as fifty years ago, the ephemeral productions of the day,—a very different thing from studying the progress or regress of the day in politics and religion. We encourage a hot-bed operatic taste that requires a strong stimulus to excite it, and consequently the delicacy of the noblest and calmest books is to us insipidity. The great secret of all delight in literature is preserving this fineness of taste, and Emerson understands it, and not only reads the great works of our own tongue, but he studies all the great inspired books of all the great literatures. He knows and reverences Shakespeare, Montaigne, and Goethe; but he has also penetrated into Plato and Confucius, into the Buddhist and Zoroastrian sacred books, which we condemn on the authority of others, without ever having looked into them ourselves, and some of which, written five hundred years before our Christian Scriptures, teach us lessons of love and forbearance, that, after eighteen hundred years have gone by, we have not yet granted the New Testament to inculcate. It seems to me that there is nothing in literature so elevating as these volumes; and we cannot help feeling how infinitely better were our time spent in really learning these, than in reading book after book of puzzling and involved commentary on a book which bears on its face that it was written for all if for any. Yet books are but little seeds after all, seeming insignificant enough before the merest weed of real life; but they lie soaking in our minds, and when we least expect it, they will spring up, not weeds, but supporters that will be our aid in the sorest struggles of our life.

2. Notes on Albert Durer[11]

If we regard any of the modern finished woodcuts, we shall find them conceived primarily in *tints* expressed by delicate lines, sometimes confused, sometimes systematic, which are individually insignificant, but collectively effect just and fine pictorial gradations. The same fact is further shown by the drawing on the block, which in the most characteristically modern cuts, as in the case of nearly all the illustrations of the popular periodicals, is almost entirely washed in with the brush; the reproduction of the smooth *tints* by systems of *lines*, being left to the discretion and technical skill of the engraver. Even when the drawing is made entirely with the pen by the artist, and the engraver merely cuts its fac-simile upon the block, we shall still find the fundamental conception to be the same, only in this case the draughtsman has endeavored in the first place to express those tints by careful shading with the pen, which in the other he left to the methods of the cutter. Albert Durer, on the other hand, contrary to the moderns, made a pen-drawing upon the block, bold and rudimentary, in which the finest gradations are not attempted, and all elaboration of tints is quite secondary to the thoughtful meaning of the individual *line*. The reason for the difference evidently lies in the improved methods and increased understanding of the material in our time. Thus, the introduction of the use of the graver on cross-cut blocks, instead of the old knife-cutting on blocks sawed along the grain, has revolutionized the technical methods of treatment; and the

---

[11]Note on Holmes's copy: "Written at the same time as the following article." The following article in Holmes's volume is *Plato*.

substitution of lines of differing thicknesses and varying proximity, instead of the old cross-hatchings, as a means of expressing shades, renders a thousand effects possible or easy that were once unattempted. Hence, our woodcuts are comparatively finished works of light and shade, in place of the sketches, perfect as they are, as such, which are the utmost results of the old art. Ruskin, who has noticed the value of Durer's line, attributes it to his profound knowledge of drawing, using the simplest means to express the most possible truth, with a material inadequate for perfect work; but if this were all, it is evident, according to Ruskin's own principles of finish, that these means ought to give all the truth consistently attainable with the material in question, whereas quite the reverse appears to be the case. In short, it is vain to deny that the reduced prominence of the single line in our cuts is the natural accompaniment of more perfectly gradated tints of color. To be sure, there were good effects from the old limitations, and indeed it was chiefly to show these that this whole comparison has been made. When each additional pen-stroke was an additional labor to the engraver, the draughtsman would take care that every line should tell as much as possible, and, giving up the delicacy to be gained by a fuller treatment, would put upon the block a severe and thoughtful drawing. Thus it is, that, as I have said, we find that with Durer every line is keen and searching as the stroke of a surgeon's knife, not one superfluous, not one to be changed but with a corresponding change of effect; so that, besides the care and thoughtfulness thus gained, there is the advantage in these old works, that finally a man shows just what he knows, and when he is ignorant must needs confess it without any of our possible disguises of uncertainty in mystery or vagueness.

Having seen the technical relations of the woodcuts of Durer to those of our own time, a matter which will be useful when we come to look at the work of three hundred years ago, let us now endeavor to determine his position as an artist.

The men of the fifteenth and sixteenth centuries, it seems to me, had one advantage not likely to be soon possessed again. Without stirring the dogmas of the Church, it is clear that a noble philosophy will suffice to teach us our duties to ourselves and our neighbors, and some may think also to our God. Some may take satisfaction in basing their moral obligations on this foundation, and in contemplating the future construction of an abstract religion on the same general ground; it is certainly now true, however, that the weaker faith of the majority of mankind prefers for these pure abstractions a clothing of more concrete fact, and demands the stimulus of a story and a life to excite their souls, sluggish to receive the highest truth; and that this demand will not remain to the end of time is by no means sure. But however this may be, certainly the growth of civilization increases our faith in the natural man, and must accordingly detract from the intense and paramount importance attached in darker times to the form of the story embodying the popular religion. Thus, while it has come to pass, that nowadays we see that duty is not less binding had the Bible never been written, or if we were to perish utterly to-morrow; on the other hand, the story that once made corporeal, and fit subject for the painter, man's highest religious conceptions,—that dramatized philosophy,—is now regarded in so far a different light, that those scenes, once wrought out with such loving faith, have now, I fear, passed from the province of art. This is something that civilization cannot restore; and neither the drooping sickliness of the modern religious painting in Germany, nor the feverish strength of all the Pre-Raphaelite religious work that I have seen, can compare with the unconscious work three centuries old and more, full of the life of the artist: thoughtful, for it came from the soul of a reformer, yet faithful, with the simple and childlike faith of early times.

But, however much be lost to art when the religious stories become matter for reasoning and scholarly dispute, in place of the old reverence of the letter, art does not finally depend for inspiration on religious form. The ideal spirit may be influenced by circumstances, but it is the great gift of humanity, not of a sect; it inspired the philosopher Plato, the artist among thinkers, as well as the Christian Durer, a thinker among artists. This it is that sees the eternal disguised in the visible form, in the particular event; and I notice that its highest results with Durer, after all, are not found in even the profound pathos and grand tenderness of the *Passion*[12] and the *Life of Christ*,[13] but in conceptions more remote from the contact of history. The mortal figures there portrayed were personal and ephemeral, but the MELANCOLIA[14] sits forever, an undecaying and immortal thought.

If we study this last-named print, we shall find it more illustrative of Durer's power, and more characteristic of his tone of thought, than perhaps any other of his works. In the anatomy of that figure there is the mass and grandeur of Michael Angelo's Night, but it is hidden under the curiously crumpling folds of the enveloping garment, elaborated with a touch of German realism; this corresponds to and illustrates the peculiar power of the artist: like that form,

---

[12]Dürer executed at least four series of *The Passion*. Holmes probably means either the series of 16 small copper engravings from 1507–1512 or the series of twelve large woodcuts from 1496–1510. *See* 2 *Albrecht Dürer 1471 bis 1528*, at 1849–64, 1522–47 (W. Hütt ed. 1971); E. Panofsky, *The Life and Art of Albrecht Dürer* 139–40, plates 186–89, 87–90, 179, 182 (1955).

[13]This may refer to one of the series of the Passion.

[14]*Melancolia I* (1514) (copper engraving); *see* 2 *Albrecht Dürer*, *supra* note 12, at 1953; E. Panofsky, *supra* note 12, at 157–71, plate 209.

massive and imposing, but like it, hiding its naked strength under the thousand folds of a disguising fancy; and if we turn to the idea of this great work, we find in it set down the history of Durer's inner life. It is full of a symbolism that we neither can entirely understand, nor wish to treat with too rude a curiosity; whatever was in Durer's mind when he wrought out the engraving, we feel, instinctively, as I have said, that into it he has thrown his life. That solitary woman is the true picture of his soul, in its strength and in its weakness; powerful, but half overcome by the many objects of its universal study; crowned with the wreath of the elect and beautiful with ideal genius, but grave with thought and marked with the care of the world; winged, yet resting sadly on the earth. Durer's genius was thoroughly German; to all its ideality there was added a realizing tendency, that makes positive his most remote and mystical fancies, in this respect recalling the criticism of Coleridge on George Herbert and the elder English poets, as "conveying the most fantastic thoughts in the most correct and natural language;" while the antithesis of the modern school, by the same author, may be quoted as also applicable to a degree in art. Of this Coleridge speaks, as "in the most fantastic language, conveying the most trivial thoughts. The latter is a riddle of words; the former, an enigma of thoughts."[15] But this last is only true of those hangers-on to a great school, who catch the mannerisms without possessing the genius of its founders.

If I have now succeeded in making plain the character of Durer's mind, it will be easy to see that in his works we may expect a wide range between those of profound imaginative thought on the one hand, and on the other, those which his love of the simplest every-day truth has prompted; and his prints and pictures may be classified according to their position between these poles. Highest would come such poems as the MELANCOLIA, which is as preferable to any scene or representation of a momentary fact as existence is higher than incident; even the *Knight and Death*,[16] though often called the greatest of his engravings, would, strictly, have to give place to this by just so much as, in the figure of the knight, it becomes lowered to the personal and individual; but there is, on the other hand, to this latter that active strength which almost forbids us to place it second to anything. The next division would contain those works which conveyed a great idea, through the medium of a person, either

---

[15]Holmes quotes, with minor alteration of punctuation, from 2 S. Coleridge, *Biographia Literaria* 73 (1962) (facsimile of 1817 ed.), which was available in many editions.

[16]*Knight, Death, and Devil* (Der Reuter) (1513) (copper engraving), not the woodcut *Death and the Knight* (1510); *see* 2 *Albrecht Dürer*, *supra* note 12, at 1592; E. Panofsky, *supra* note 12, at 151–55, plate 207.

actually or conceivably historical; as in the almost awed expression, as of man rising from the experience of the other world, and yet the look of Godlike benignity, portrayed in the face of Christ (strangely contrasting with the animal immobility of the sleeping guards), in the woodcut of the Resurrection in the *Lesser Passion*.[17] A different example of the same class is the *War-Horse*, of which a good copy on wood was published by Charles Blanc, in the *History of the Painters of all Nations*,[18] the same cut being republished in the Illustrated Magazine of Art, for January, 1854. Only lower than the just mentioned Resurrection in the capacity of the subject, perhaps greater in power of treatment, is the larger woodcut of Christ sinking under the cross;[19] to judge of Raphael's similar picture[20] by engravings, the older print is as far superior in sincerity, in sentiment, and in grandeur, as it is in vivid reality, and this though Raphael had probably seen either it, or the similar one of the smaller series, before he began his painting. Thus, through the second division there would be a gradual descent, marked by the decrease of the higher qualities, through the works containing appeals to the nobler human feelings but approaching nearer to every-day life, such as many of the cuts in the *Life of the Virgin*,[21] down, finally, to purely unimaginative statement of fact.

The above classification is the best one, I believe, of so general a nature, and though, of course, not absolute, points out a principle applicable in ranking the works and in settling the position of all artists. There are various considerations, however, which act as drawbacks; thus, we have already seen that certain qualities in the *Knight and Death* caused us to value it as little inferior to the MELANCOLIA, nay, in some respects superior, though the presumption was in favor of the superiority of the latter. We can,

---

[17]*The Small Passion* (published 1511) was a series of thirty-seven woodcuts. *The Resurrection* of the series was cut *ca*. 1509. *See* 2 *Albrecht Dürer*, *supra* note 12, at 1590–1629; E. Panofsky, *supra* note 12, at 139–45, plates 190–94.

[18]Three different editions of this work appeared in English translation—one in 1852 and two in 1853.

[19]*Bearing of the Cross* (ca. 1497–1498), from the series of twelve woodcuts *The Large Passion* (1511); *see* 2 *Albrecht Dürer*, *supra* note 12, at 1536; E. Panofsky, *supra* note 12, plate 89.

[20]*The Spasimo do Sicilia* (*ca*. 1516) is a large canvas depicting Simon coming to the aid of Jesus, bearing the cross. It is now believed that Raphael's assistants Penni and Giulio executed much of the painting. *See* Marabottini, *Raphael's Collaborators*, in *The Complete Works of Raphael* 247–48 (1969).

[21]*Life of the Virgin* (published 1511) (series of twenty woodcuts); *see* 2 *Albrecht Dürer*, *supra* note 12, at 1548–89; E. Panofsky, *supra* note 12, at 96–194, plates 86, 141–44. 181.

again, easily fancy it possible that the magnificent vitality of Titian might be worth more than any less healthy, though more aspiring work; and, in the same way, the majestic grace of Raphael might very probably outweigh profounder thought expressed in the coarser forms of Durer. To speak about such different qualities relatively is as hard as to compare the commanding power of a great statesman with the more abstract ability of the philosopher; the one conveys the greater sense of power, yet in the other we recognize the higher range of thought; the best we can do is to fix on an intermediate point, where the keen eye and directing brain of the man of the world keep more abstract reflection from falling into weakness. One thing I think we can say; just as the lowest form of good art is the mere portraiture of the single, unconnected fact, with no further view beyond,—like the painting of the nosegay, for instance, with the decay, the worm, and the dew-drop set down with equal faithfulness,—so art is great in proportion as it rises above this, and the presumption is always in favor of that picture being greatest in which the lower truth of the individual is made subservient (notice, I do not say falsified or even neglected, but made subservient) to the profounder truth of the idea. Knowledge of the stains of the earth, and of the decay that accompanies all earthly life, doubtless the painter needs, but higher than this is the sight which beholds the type disguised beneath the wasting form, and higher than anything connected with the individual is the conception of the harmonious whole of a great work, and this again is great, just as its idea partakes of what is eternal. And this striving to look on types and eternal ideas, is that highest gift of the artist, which is called the ideal tendency.

I had hoped finally to have devoted a few words to Durer in his wider relations, as a man who resumed in himself and represents in his works the great tendencies of his age and country, but the limited space forbids. As it is, all that I have attempted, has been to hint at that combination of noble powers, coming at a thoughtful time, that have made his works dearer to me, and more valued instructors than any book and than any other art.

3. Alma Mater[22]

(Read at the Sophomore Supper of the Class of '61.)
Two years have passed since fair Harvard received us, —
Two years touched the face of our smiling young earth, —
She who with many a pang has conceived us,
Two years from now will give some of us birth;

---

[22]This poem was previously published with a few minor mistakes, in M. Howe, *supra* note 1, at 50. The text in S. Novick, *Honorable Justice: The Life of Oliver Wendell Holmes* 26 (1989), is incomplete.

And we shall love her,
Our bountiful mother,
We shall all love her, wherever we go;
Both for her motherhood,
And for our brotherhood,
We shall all love her, wherever we go.

Babies in life, we shall play with its roses,
Boys, see their opening; men, watch their decay;
But the beauty imparting a higher discloses,
And we find the fruit just as the flower drops away.
Then drink to our mother,
Our bountiful mother,
For we shall love her, wherever we go;
Both for her motherhood
And for our brotherhood
We shall all love her, wherever we go.

4. Plato[23]

Socrates, who is continually before our eyes as forming the nucleus of the Platonic dialogues, and as the foundation which furnished them their stability and weight, is known to us chiefly through the colored medium of those writings; and when we also include the humbler memoirs of his other pupil, Xenophon, we have the chief authorities for his life and teachings. In connection with Plato, then, he stands like one of the Blue Hills: the roots and base of the unyielding rock, but covered with the growth of forests and the accumulations of centuries, clothing and softening the contours of its rough ribs and only here and there the stern lines of the massive core showing unmistakably to the sky. As far as possible let us first settle the character and relation of this nucleus to the later growth which has enveloped it.

Socrates does not appear to have been a systematic philosopher; the dogmas he enunciated were few and uncertain. He was a rough old citizen with a big brain, who, belonging at Athens, and exceeding even his countrymen in his making man the proper centre of human thought, occupies himself in asking all sorts of questions of everybody with regard to matters practically interesting to men.[24] Here is a

---

[23]Note on Holmes's copy: "Took the prize for the year 1860. Written in the summer vacation 1860."

[24]Note on Holmes's copy: "Memorabilia Δ VII." TΔhis is a citation to Xenophon, *Memorabilia*, bk. 4, ch. 7, where Xenophon recounted how Socrates taught his students to acquire knowledge of subjects like geometry and astronomy that were of practical application in activities like surveying and navigating.

condensed translation from the Theatetus of a passage wherein he speaks of himself and his province: "Have you not then heard that I am the son of the very noble and reverend midwife, Phaenarete, and that I follow the same profession? Consider all the relations of midwifery and you will more easily see what I mean. For you know that no one at the time of conception and pregnancy delivers others, but those who are past that period; and is it not evident that midwives more than others have the power to distinguish those really pregnant and those who are not?—Now in other respects my art of midwifery resembles theirs, but it differs in that it delivers men not women, and has regard to pregnant souls, not bodies; *and in this point I am like the midwives; I am barren of wisdom, and that which many have taunted me with, that I question others but give no answer myself on any subject, is a true reproach.*[25] The cause being that the Deity compels me to act the part of midwife, but has prevented me from myself bringing forth. *I am not, therefore, at all wise, nor have I any discovery that is the offspring of my own mind.* But of those who associate with me, some appear at first very ignorant, but all, as our intimacy advances, if the Deity grants it, show such a wonderful proficiency that it is evident to all. And this clearly without learning anything from me, but of themselves discovering and becoming possessed of many beautiful and noble thoughts."[26]

Though Socrates often uses these statements of his as a sly cover for an impending confutation, he still was perfectly in earnest as to the fact.[27] His peculiar power lay not so much in a profound perception of truth as in a natural spirit of argumentative questioning, which he developed into his system of dialectics, demanding the initiatory definition, which it is also his claim to have introduced, as the necessary first step. He had a bent not too speculative and ideal to prevent his avowing the amelioration of

---

[25]Note on Holmes's copy: "Gorg. 506A." At *Gorgias* 506a Socrates discussed his method of argument and disclaimed any pretense to special knowledge. Robert Stoddart has brought to my attention the fact that, despite what Socrates said about method in this passage, his actual procedure in the passage was exceptional. Because Kallikles would not argue with Socrates, Socrates elaborated answers himself from his own questions.

[26]*Theaetetus* 149a–150d. Holmes omitted much material, which is not indicated by ellipses.

[27]Note on Holmes's copy: "1, Grote, Plato Ch. VI. VII 292." George Grote's twelve-volume *A History of Greece* appeared in London in 1846–1856, and there were numerous English and American versions by 1860. But G. Grote, *Plato, and Other Companions of Socrates*, 3 volumes, did not appear until 1865, and Holmes studied the latter in 1867. His diary recorded that he finished volume 3 on September 24, 1867. Holmes Diary for 1867, Holmes Papers, Harvard Law School Library, manuscript box 19, folder 2.

present institutions as the ultimate purpose of his questions, rather than any more remote love of truth as such.[28] Taking a subject bearing on the education of youth, perhaps, or, as in the Theaetetus, propounding a question on the nature of science, he would easily obtain from his companion some definition,[29] loosely thought out, as might be expected from the unscientific use of language and lax thought of that time, and then would proceed with fatal effect[30] to apply the proffered garment to the form it was to fit, and prove it here too short, there too full, and in another place again too tight to meet its destined end.

Many of the dialogues most representative of the real Socrates come to an end, having only indicated by negations a positive opinion, and others give us no clue to his idea of the truth; and indeed very likely he had no clear idea of it, but was working after his obstetric fashion to see if he could not elicit it from some other mind. But when Socrates did undertake to arrive at the truth constructively, his chief means was by the fallacious argument drawn from single analogies;[31] a plausible analogy furnished to his mind proof all-sufficient and conviction to every doubt, and when it was once in his grasp he held on to it until he had pressed from it every germ of possible suggestion. The resemblance of principle ratios being settled, he would unhesitatingly assume the same likeness in all minor points without being startled by any result that might be induced by the process. It is thus in an example from the same part of the Theaetetus that I have previously quoted from, which I use merely as it happens to be nearest at hand, though in other cases results far more illogical and in some instances even shocking to sound morality occur. In this instance he merely trivially argues from a recognized similarity between the midwife and the reaper of grain that, because, as he assumes, the reaper should also know the proper seed to be sown in various soil,[32] therefore the midwife should know as part of her business the becoming mates in marriage for the various

---

[28]Notes on Holmes's copy: "Gorg[ias] 521 D." and "Memorabilia Δ VII."

[29]Note on Holmes's copy: "Definition, Division &c. in Phaedrus 265: A, B." At that passage Socrates subdivided the definition of love into different types of love.

[30]Note on Holmes's copy: "Method Gorg. 464A.478D [τo] καλὸν [accent sic] [the good] defined)." At *Gorgias* 474 Socrates elicited a preliminary opinion from Polus that it is better to suffer wrong than to do wrong. Through leading questions Socrates showed Polus the error of the opinion.

[31]Note on Holmes's copy: "Imperf. analogy. Gorg. 478.A; 480.B." *Gorgias* 478a, 478b compared justice and medicine and drew inferences about justice from the practice of medicine.

[32]Holmes's copy changes "soil" to "soils."

temperaments. It is not an important point, nor does Socrates make it so, but it will illustrate the fact.

> "*Socr.*—Didn't you know this about them, that they are most skillful matchmakers, as being competent to distinguish from what unions will spring the finest children?
>
> *Theaet.*—I did not altogether know that.
>
> *Socr.*—*** Consider; do you think that the cultivation and gathering of the fruits of the earth, and again the knowledge of the proper soil for the various plants and seeds, belong to the same or a different art?
>
> *Theaet.*—Certainly to the same." (In the first part of this analogy, even, we have a fallacy, for a reaper may clearly be competent for[33] his business and know nothing of planting or cultivation.)
>
> "*Socr.* —But with regard to women, my friend, do you think there is one art of adapting the seed to the soil and another of gathering the fruit?
>
> *Theaet.*—It is not reasonable to suppose so."[34]

Just as personally he was a wonder of physical endurance, able to walk barefoot through the snow at a temperature which his fellow-soldiers could hardly bear, wrapt in their warm fur coverings, and undergoing all hardships without a complaint, or even the appearance of suffering, so was Socrates characterized mentally by an enormous vitality. This did not fail him in his latest hours, but gave him that confidence which enabled him to face his death with such calm dignity; and the same activity of mind which led to his questions and his public cross-examinations must have imparted to his conversations a vigor that,[35] with the sense of his moral strength, probably did much to gain over and retain for him the many pupils who attended his daily steps.

Having now seen, as well as the brief space allows, the philosophical position of Socrates, as a man rather of a keen and caustic spirit of enquiry, than of great constructive power, and naturally therefore the one to introduce definition and logical induction from more or less accurate premises; as a man whose more practical turn of mind and unflinching moral courage, as well as physical daring, seem to have been a foundation that was needed for the speculative superstructure reared by his chief pupil; let us, without undertaking the uncertain task of settling the distinctive dogmas of the master's creed, turn our attention to Plato, who, being

---

[33]Holmes's copy changes "for" to "to."

[34]*Theaetetus* 149d–150a.

[35]Holmes's copy changes "that" to "which."

apparently more devoted to purely abstract speculation, seems to have embraced all the positive opinions of Socrates, aiding them by new arguments and illustrations, and who has certainly also added new ones peculiar to himself;[36] Plato, moreover, who was fully in our sense of the word a philosopher, has arranged and perfected the conversational method of Socrates into a delicate and powerful instrument of exact written thought, and has obtained the best results possible to be gained by its means. In addition to all this, he gives life and breath to all his dialectics by the animation of his dramatic power and the grandeur of the poetic allegory.

In speaking of Socrates, I have briefly explained the peculiar logical method which Plato received from his master, and aided and enlarged by the addition of a more rigid analysis. Now with the first of the two the method was all in all, as it gave a systematic order to his daily conversations; and though by its means truth was brought to light, yet still it was with the delivering of the person in labor, not with the child when fairly in the world, that he was especially concerned. Plato, however, the scientific lecturer, (though he too set a value on dialectic skirmishing merely as such,) had aspirations also to positive theories; among these the most prominent is the famous but sometimes misinterpreted Theory of Ideas, and this, as the basis of his system, I will now endeavor to explain.

Everything material has of course certain qualities by which it is characterized; as for instance, that of beauty—a deer, a landscape, and a man, might all, though very unlike, be rightly called beautiful—moreover, there is the higher beauty of the soul, and still higher, one of science.

What is it that makes it right to apply the same adjective to all of these? It is, answers Plato, generalizing, because in an ascending scale all of these partake and more and more nearly approach the abstract *idea of beauty*; 'which is eternal, being neither produced nor destroyed, and suffering neither increase nor decay, which is not beautiful at one point or at one time only and not at another, nor beautiful in the eyes of some but not so to others; nor is this beauty an outward appearance merely, like a face or a hand or anything corporeal, nor is it any discourse or science, nor does it exist anywhere in any being, nor in any point in space; but it subsists by and with itself in eternal unity. And all other things are beautiful in so far as they partake of this, and in such a way that while everything else is subject to birth and decay, it suffers no change and is liable to no casualty.'

Man is man, again Plato also says, just so far as he partakes of humanity, and a table so far as it partakes of the tabular idea. But

---

[36]Holmes's copy changes the semicolon to a comma.

here, as it seems to me, there is a serious confusion introduced into the system, owing to the admitting equally, without distinction, the simple ideas like those on which mathematical truth is dependent, or perhaps, like beauty, which alone are recognized by our intuitive faculty, (and which, with Plato, we may suppose necessary ideas permanently existing in the mind of the Creator,) and the *complex* conceptions of table and chair, which are evidently mere arbitrary combinations effected by man; or still further, those like *humanity*, which is a purely general statement, drawn from observation, of a *present* fact, equally as far as we know, dependent on the arbitrary will of the Deity. In other words, more briefly, as long as we have faith in reason we must believe in the truths of mathematics and the like existing as absolute necessities in the nature of things, while we see, at least, no such necessary existence for the ideas humanity, table &c.; and Plato was wrong, therefore, in characterizing both the classes as absolute and as equally ὀυτως ὀυτα.*[37]

A convenient illustration of the above theory might be offered in the shape of a diagram.

Let us suppose from a common focus the principal axes of many ellipses to radiate in all directions; the various nature of the different ellipses depends entirely on the relation of the separate foci, (which to our view may represent the centres of individuality,) to the common

---

[37]Holmes's copy corrects ὀυτως ὀυτα to ὀντως ὀντα (actually existing [things] or substance.]

[*Footnote * to the article:*]

> The above is meant to be so stated as to be true in outline to sensationalist and idealist alike; for, without entering into the distinctions of necessary and contingent truth, it is evident that mathematics express the simplest relations of all created things, whereas creation might conceivably have stopped short of man or man not have invented a table. But it is especially the including of the idea table, which no sensationalists of the present time would call of the same order, in the same category with those connected with mathematical truth or beauty that stamps the unscientific character of his theory.
>
> Since the above words were written and the whole essay finished and put into other hands, a new volume by Whewell, on the Philosophy of Discovery,' has appeared, in which the same criticism is made, in language so similar that I insert the passage here; "But Plato seems, in many of his writings, to extend this doctrine much further; and he assumed not only Ideas of Space and its properties, from which geometrical truths are derived; but of Relations, as the Relations of Like and Unlike, Greater and Less; and of mere material objects, as Tables and Chairs. Now to assume Ideas of such thing as these solves no difficulty and is supported by no argument. In this respect the Ideal Theory is of no value in Science." pp. 12,13. It is pleasant to find one's self sustained by such high authority.

[Holmes quotes, with minor changes, W. Whewell, *On the Philosophy of Discovery: Chapters Historical and Critical* 12–13 (1860).]

central focus which stands for the Platonic abstraction, and which, although the essential point common to all the ellipses, is, nevertheless, only a geometrical idea destitute of extension or any predicable qualities. The ratio of the focus of individuality to this central point, is, I say, the essential matter; and the ellipse, a figure having extension, yet depending for its character on an idea, precisely represents the relation, according to the theory of Plato, of a beautiful object to the abstract quality, beauty. Now beauty, Plato likewise holds, is the most sensible presentation of the Good, which is the definition, so to speak, of God, and which embraces all the other permanent representative ideas. The Good is the end of all philosophy, and as this is attained to by the study of the various ideas which represent it and which it comprehends, such study is philosophy, is Science *par excellence*.

Dialectic, therefore, or Logic, as concerned with these immutable ideas, which alone, as he holds, owing to their immutability, admit of definition, is exalted to this position, and science founded on observation, as concerned with mutable matters, must take an entirely secondary place. But Logic is, in fact, merely an instrument which works with data previously obtained, whether from this very physical science or from intuition; and the unhappy fallacy in connection with this point, that is, with regard to its functions, which runs all through Plato, is that he confounds this drawing of conclusions already contained in the premise, by Logic, which can only develop a preexisting statement, with the finding of new data or statements, for which we must look to consciousness or to generalizations from experience. Moreover*[38] all logical investigation into the nature of the subject of a statement or definition, is only good so far as the definition may be supposed absolutely and not only relatively true; and yet Plato, in common with others of the ancients, assuming a definition which will only stand in the capacity of showing the meaning *he attaches* to the word to be the true expression of the actual fact referred to by it, proceeds thence to deduce consequences relative to the essential nature of the fact.

---

[38][*Footnote * to the article:*]

> This latter point I first found noticed in Lewes's Biogr. Hist. of Philosophy; (library ed. London, p. 130). *See also* Devey's Logic, Bohn 'Nominal Definition mistaken, &c.' p. 73. Lewes also was the first, as far as I know, to point out the difference of the Socratic and Baconian induction; I have used these points as aiding in establishing conclusions originally founded on the study of Plato himself.

[Works cited are: G. Lewes, *A Biographical History of Philosophy* (London ed. 1857) and J. Devey, *Logic: Or the Science of Inference* (1854).]

As I have made use of this prominent example of beauty in illustrating Plato's Ideal Theory, it may be worth while to try to explain, before leaving the subject, the real nature of the famous Platonic Love, which is connected with this idea of the beautiful.[39]

Love is the faculty by which we immediately apprehend the Good, of which, as has been said, beauty is the most sensible presentation. Every being that is mortal desires and earnestly strives to partake of these verities which are alone immortal; and this striving after immortality, in the lowest organisms, takes the forms of mere animal desire for procreation. Those, however, who feel desire in their souls, have as their proper offspring intellect and every other excellence, of which poets and inventors are the chief generators. Now when any one of a really divine soul arrives at maturity, he longs earnestly to beget an offspring; and being unwilling to generate upon what is ugly, seeks ardently for a beautiful object. And if he meets another beautiful and noble soul, especially if it have also a finely moulded body to match, he rushes to embrace this combination, and, discoursing much on virtue, he, acting as teacher, endeavors to direct his pupil in the path of his duty, and to bring up those immortal children, (beautiful and noble thoughts,) which any one who might choose would prefer to those of mortal birth. Platonic Love is, in more modern language, the association of two noble souls, master and pupil, in the bonds of affection, for the purpose of encouraging a higher morality, a profounder perception of truth and a more real inward beauty.

I have spoken thus at length about this Theory of Ideas and the matters connected with it, because these ideas are the pillars on which Plato's system stands, and because by discovering, as far as possible, the strength and weakness of his foundation, we can infer the soundness of the whole structure. What has been the result of our investigation? We have seen that the fundamental classification of the ideas was loose and unscientific;[40] that Plato's conception of the true method of investigating their nature was vague and incorrect; and, to cap the climax, we need only to have studied his works to know the extreme difficulty of fixing on any exact and consistent opinion as steadily held to by him. I believe that his notion of the relation of the material individual form to the εἶδος, the type or species, varied at

---

[39]Note on Holmes's copy: "Symposium 205.B." At *Symposium* 205–206 Socrates recounted Diotima's understanding of love as a yearning to conceive and generate the good or beautiful.

[40]Note on Holmes's copy: "II Ritter Ch. 3 end." 2 H. Ritter, *The History of Ancient Philosophy* 332–37 (A. Morrison trans. 1838).

different times;[41] he even left room for dispute as to exactly what he thought with regard to the central matter, and has furnished texts for the extremest realists, as well as to those of more moderate views. And after the best pains that we take to find him out, there are many ready to inform us that our labor is quite vain, for all that we can gather from these writings is but exoteric doctrine, whereas his esoteric opinion was transmitted only by word of mouth to his disciples: in this latter statement, however, founded chiefly on an equivocal expression of Aristotle, I do not put the least faith, since that which we have offered us in the dialogues is exactly such as we should have expected from one of Plato's natural constitution, reacting on the method and teachings received from his masters, and since there is only too great a willingness to give credit to all remote persons and times for unattainable and hidden superiorities.

From the above results we may fairly conclude, I think, that the constructive system of Plato, confused and doubtful as it is, though a vast step as introducing more accurate and well defined thought than had previously existed, has for us no scientific value whatsoever. It needed a complete remodelling before it would suffice as a consistent cosmology. This point, which will be briefly explained in another place, we must, I think, concede, and I wish especially to insist upon it, because there is a continual unscientific neglect of the history of the progress of thought in our ordinary way of looking back upon past time; in which we seem like infants grasping vaguely at remote objects, with no power to distinguish them from those near at hand. Swedenborgianism, admirable as it is in its philosophy of human life, is peculiarly guilty in this point, looking back and quoting Pythagoras, and relying much on esoteric doctrine, not seeing that from the entire absence of the central idea of science, it was impossible for the people of that time, to have held secrets that the world has not yet caught up with, or rather has entirely fallen away from. Our chemists do know really more than the best of the alchymists, and it is not worth troubling ourselves now much about their elixirs and their philosopher's stone,*[42] and so with the ancient metaphysicians, we may spend much time in looking for what they never had, and for what the whole order of things forbade their

---

[41]Note on Holmes's copy: "Cf. Ritter loc. cit. Was matter itself ideal?—p. 319. That it is the μὴ ὄν [nonbeing thing]." *See id.* at 318–21 (critical discussion of Plato's idealist treatment of material objects).

[42][*Footnote * to the article:*]

> As an example on the other side might be offered the splendid structures of Egypt and of Baalbec, but these very structures owed their magnificence to a semi-barbarian disregard of the life of the lower classes on the part of those in power.

having; but more of this further on. But now, abandoning that exactness of science which Plato lived too early to attain, let us wonder at the profound insight into all nature, the instinct for great truth, which he displays. His allegorical presentation of the soul, in the Phaedrus, as a charioteer driving two horses, the one of noble birth and beautiful, the other base and struggling with the reins, and the charioteer, as long as he can command the latter, remaining in the contemplation of the eternal verities and of God; but, losing that control, being forced to sink to an earthly body, while the twelve gods drive calmly on forever, and the rest: how sublimely does it set forth the conditions of human life! Indeed, as has just been noticed of Swedenborg, where Plato is supernatural, and deals with demons and with other states of being, he is most supremely natural; as the "Heaven and Hell," though we may not accept it as revelation, is not less wonderful if we are content to apply it to this world for its explanation of relations here.

Moreover, in separating man the idea, from man the concrete, how completely Plato has anticipated the best art by dividing the accidental from the real. How deeply would he have felt the difference of the plodder, who, professing[43] nature as his model, puts before him a flower, and copies every corrosion and chance stain upon its leaves, (not that such art may not have its place,) and the great artist, who seizing the type of the plant, paints that upon his canvas, and leaves the rest in the subordination in which it belongs. When the admirable artist of the *White Captive*[44] said that in every man and woman he

---

[43]Holmes's copy inserts "to take" here.

[44]The American artist Erastus Dow Palmer displayed a number of marble sculptures in New York in 1856, which aroused much public interest. "The New York exhibition spread Palmer's reputation far beyond his native state [New York]. Particularly gratifying was a letter asking him to exhibit his work in Boston, for it was signed by such distinguished names as Everett, Sparks, Agassiz, Longfellow, Prescott, Lowell." M. Thorp, *The Literary Sculptors* 146–47 (1965). *See also* A. Gardner, *Yankee Stonecutters* 32–33 (1945); Ingraham, *Erastus Dow Palmer, A Great American Sculptor, Americana* 7–21 (1930). In the late 1850s Palmer sculpted *The White Captive* in marble. (It is now in the American Wing at the Metropolitan Museum of Art.)

The White Captive portrays a standing female nude with her arms bound behind her to a stake. The appeal of the bound female nude had been exploited in 1845 by Hiram Powers's marble *The Greek Slave*. For a psychoanalytic and historical discussion of Powers's work, *see* P. Gay, *The Bourgeois Experience: Victoria to Freud* 396–402 (1984). *The Greek Slave* caused considerable moral and critical controversy during its exhibition in America in 1847. *See generally* M. Thorp, *supra*, at 73, 116–22; A. Gardner, *supra*, at 14–16. Holmes was familiar with the controversy of the nudes, because in 1859 "public outcry forced the Boston Athanaeum to remove from tried to see their face and form as it would have been if it had descended from Adam, still characteristic, but free from the marks of sins and sickness, he was talking pure Platonism and true art.

What, again, is more profound than his perception of the fatality attaching to matter?[45] With it the law of cause and effect is absolute; if we know the data, the results are inevitable; only self-determining vital centres are free from this necessary consequence and fix on this or that for no cause except that such was their will. Matter represents the limits of our thoughts, and is the evil necessity which the free soul, inclined to virtue so far as it is free and still wise, must overcome. Heaven, the world of the absolute ideas and the pure spirits, cannot, consistently with the goodness of God, contain evil, and its[46] existence is consequently found to be in this gross matter, veiling the ideas and deadening the perception of the spirit. Hence the philosopher's is, in Plato's estimation, the highest pursuit among mortals;[47] for what is philosophy but a preparation for death, or the

---

exhibition on its walls William Page's *Venus Guiding Aeneas*." M. Thorp, *supra*, at 23. Daguerreotype and other reproductions of Palmer's work were widely available. A. Gardner, *supra*, at 33.

Palmer's sculpture was less classical than Powers's in style and theme. The native aspects of the sculpture were emphasized in an anonymous fantasy on the work *Palmer's "White Captive,"* 5 *Atlantic Monthly* Jan. 1860, at 108–09, which opined that "White Captive' proves its claim to genuine greatness, and . . . it will presently take its place, with the world's consent, in the front rank of modern statues,—good among the best, in the flesh-and-bloodness and the soul of it. It is original, it is faithful, it is American."

I have been unable to identify the source of the statement that Holmes attributed to Palmer. If Holmes refers to Palmer's writing, the citation must be to *Philosophy of the Ideal, The Crayon* (January 1856), Palmer's only published essay. Thorp, *supra*, at 147. The views attributed to Palmer are not expressed in that essay, but they are very similar to those expressed by Powers. *See* 1 C. Lester, *The Artist, the Merchant, and the Statesman, of the Age of Medici and of our own Times* 99–100 (1845) (transcript of conversations with Powers). Holmes may have been confusing the two artists.

I am grateful to Dr. Susan P. Casteras for suggesting that Holmes was referring to a sculptor, not to an English or Pre-Raphaelite painting as I had assumed.

[45]Note on Holmes's copy: "Tim. 68.d. 56.c." At *Timaeus* 56c, 68d Plato referred to God's combination of invisibly small material parts so as to produce the phenomenal effects of the objective world; but Plato assumed that one could neither understand nor experience the process.

[46]Holmes's copy underlines "its" and contains a note, "What's?"—referring to the ambiguous reference.

[47]Note on Holmes's copy: "Phaedo, 82–83 &d. Gorg. 526. G. Theaet. 173.D. to 177.C."

anticipation of the time when we shall be rid of those blinds of the flesh which interpose between us and wisdom.

If we could see to-day the telescope constructed by Galileo, with its clumsy tube and simple lenses, ground, perhaps, by his own hand, with what reverence should we handle that primitive instrument, with what feelings should we gaze up through it at the satellites of Jupiter first discovered by its means! But if we desired to study the mysteries which perplex the astronomer of to-day, we should very certainly seek an instrument which the latest perfections of science had best adapted to our needs. We should not, therefore, detract from the glory of him who first revealed the mighty powers hidden in what previously had been known only as an amusing toy; nor would he be less great because his successors, following in his footsteps, had attained results which he could never have anticipated[48] by means of instruments which had superseded his own. We are too apt to forget those accumulations of new material, and[49] consequent correction or annulling of old results and methods in every branch of knowledge, which, with the steady advances of civilization, each eager generation continually makes.

Galileo's telescope, doubled, is our opera-glass; and as it has been with the astronomer, so also has it been with Plato, the explorer in different realms. While he remains the original interpreter of certain primary facts and relations of the human spirit to the central and eternal ideas, he still bears to us the same relation that a self-made man does to one who has been bred in the midst of riches, and educated from his earliest youth; the circumstances of the former may even have aided to display and develop his natural powers, (and genius at any rate needs but few materials to work with,) but certainly the latter starts with an advantage which can never be annulled, whatever may be his inferiority in natural parts.

We start far beyond the place where Plato rested. He lived too early to be able to avail himself of the history of the fluctuations in philosophy, to aid in shaping his own conceptions of philosophical truth; and[50] far more important, and what should continually be taken into account in estimating his views, it is only in these last days that anything like an all-comprehending science has embraced the universe, showing unerring law prevailing in every department, generalizing and systematizing every phenomenon of physics, and every vagary of the human mind. Plato, having raised to an exquisite perfection the instrument of dialectics which he received from his master, was led thereby to the most noble and remote of his

---

[48]Holmes's copy inserts a comma here.

[49]Holmes's copy inserts "the" here.

[50]Holmes's copy inserts "what is" here and deletes the following "what."

discoveries, though scientifically imperfect as we have seen[51]—the Theory of Ideas. When he had laid this result before the world he had done all that with his facilities was possible, and was of necessity compelled to wait for a more extended experience, and more perfect instruments to exceed his farthest vision and embrace in a wider science his boldest generalizations; and when he undertook the construction of a Republic[52] from the few data which he could attain, he was laboring as vainly as one who should endeavor to find the successive actual positions of the moon from his mathematical knowledge, being ignorant of the solar perturbations, and the motion of the nodes and apsides; and yet, owing to the comparative obscurity of the subject, we see his crudest ideas discussed to-day with a gravity of which the Ptolemaic system is now equally worthy.

In quitting this subject,[53] on which free criticism as well as praise has been used, I should wish my last words to be those of the reverence and love with which this great man and his master always fill me; it seems to me that on the subjects that[54] are the highest, and also the most difficult, few final *results* are yet attained; I do not feel sure that each man's own experience is not always to be that which must ultimately settle his belief, but to see a really great and humane spirit fighting the same fights with ourselves, and always preserving an ideal faith and a manly and heroic conduct; doubly recommended, moreover, to our hearts by the fact of his having only himself to rely on, and no accepted faith that killed a doubt it did not answer; the spectacle, I say, of these two grand old heathen,[55] the master the inspired fighter, the scholar the inspired thinker, fills my heart with love and reverence at one of the grandest sights the world can boast.

5. Editors' Table

We read in the papers, that at the Alumni dinner Mr. T.W. Higginson gave as a sentiment, "*The Harvard Magazine*: May it have a new usefulness, long life, and *almost* as many subscribers as the Atlantic."

---

[51]Holmes's copy inserts a comma here.

[52]Note on Holmes's copy: "That P. did not conceive his Rep. purely ideal—cf. II Ritter 420. [2 H. Ritter, *supra* note 40, at 420.] Rep. IX. 5092a. VI 501–e. [Republic citations are to XI 592a and VI 50k.] [Illegible.]"

[53]Holmes's copy underlines the word "subject" in this and the preceding sentence to indicate the repetition.

[54]Holmes's copy changes "that" to "which." *See also supra*, note 35. The proper use of "that" and "which" was something that continued to perplex Holmes, and he later corresponded with Pollock on the subject. *See* 1 Holmes-Pollock Letters 131 (M. Howe ed. 1942).

[55]Holmes's copy changes "heathen" to "heathens."

For this kind wish, coming just as the new debutants are making their first and naturally timid bow, they feel, of course, a gratitude as real as this demonstration of good-will, from one not immediately and personally interested in the support of the Magazine, was unexpected. And yet the very unexpected nature of the toast suggests to the editors a wish that it were not quite so tacitly assumed that a College periodical could have no interest outside of the College walls. The common assumption, that nothing but matters connected with students, as such, have here a fitting place, contributes to this impression; whereas the true statement should rather be, that the preponderance of such subjects gives the *Harvard* its distinctive tone as a College magazine, just as the opening offered to every student to speak *any* sincere opinion imparts to it its greatest value. If it were our rule never to let anything, however slight, escape from our hand into print but what was the result of our life and experience *so far*, the lightest pieces, as well as the most solid, would still find equal place; but the detestable flippancy of College slang would be avoided, while all the real wit and peculiar humor of youth would appear the more evident by the destruction of its disguises. If this were done, though new *results* would not probably be displayed to the world, *tendencies*, which, in almost every man, are more important, would be shown, and we should be free from the dread of a future shame at these productions, which no one would rightly feel as the true exponent of a certain stage of development. Moreover, an increased sincerity in fun, as well as in more serious productions, would not fail to excite that degree of attention in the surrounding world, that seems to us but the *Harvard's* proper due;—not great, of course, but merely a proper respect for the expressions of our thought and sentiment, instead of the contempt which youthful flippancy is so sure to inspire. In offering these remarks, however, the editors would not be understood as finding proofs of what unearnest people like to call "earnestness" in heavy subject; there is not even much presumption in favor of the superiority of an essay so mounted, but evidence is to be drawn only from the matter of the piece, and the question is, Did the author write with an intention?

To do their utmost in conducting to such writing, in place of articles only intended to fill a vacancy, the editors wish, once for all, to solicit *voluntary* contributions from *all the classes*, to prevent, as far as possible, that compulsory, hurried, and probably, therefore bad writing, which is too apt to be the result of a promise hastily made and ill kept. As assurance, moreover, of an unbiased judgment on the contributions that may be offered, the editors have determined that each number shall be published under the care and supervision of the whole board; thinking, also, that by this means there will be prevented that limitation of the contributions to a single class—

alternating as the editor for the month was Senior or Junior—that ensued under a different method. Finally, as the editors on their part promise a diligent care (for which, observe, they gain literally no remuneration), the least that the students can do, if they choose to elect editors for the continuance of the Magazine, is to contribute their annual two dollars to its support; and we would also signify to those now Alumni, that they too, as they praise, may well drop their mite into the coffers of the *Harvard*.

6. Editors' Table

In this number will be found recorded the annual victory of the Harvard boats in the College Union Regatta of last July. For two beautiful days Worcester was overflowing with the student life that filled its hotels and streets; confident Cambridge men and more doubtful Yale, with the rarer few from other colleges. In the soul of one from Cambridge everything was calculated to inspire satisfaction and delight. The enthusiastic bets, somewhat wild in the eyes of the more prudent, that on the first day Harvard won every race, brought in to the adventurous that solid assurance of the right direction things were taking that opened the hearts of the happy ones to extraneous joys; for such, the song did not unrequited woo, with nocturnal blandishments, sleep from their embrace. Such even the harmless but expensive pleasures of Worcesterian cabbage-leaf did not in vain allure; the Cantabrigians were happy;—nor were all others sad, but rather each after his kind, whether on the winning or the losing side, shared in the general jollity.

We cannot here detail the events that then took place,—the chess, the billiards, the songs of the Glee Club, the feats of individual prowess, nor even the meeting of sad-eyed editors, though we may mention the fact that the resolutions of their general conclave as to the University Quarterly will be printed on a separate sheet for distribution; and though we might become critical on some minor points, as for instance at the too easy down-heartedness of the Yale Sophs, on the second day, for men of real pluck, at the accidental impeding of their course by our Sophomore boat, still it is not worth while so to disturb the pleasant retrospect offered in those two days.

One matter, however, not set down in the record, yet as justly to be catalogued against us as our better parts to be noted in our favor, needs a mention here. We refer, of course, to the general rowdyism of demeanor shown by the students. We can but say *general*, for the most public demonstrations of this sort were participated in by a large majority of the collegians present; and that their conduct was only to be characterized as *rowdyism*, any one who was there, and will forget the special fact of who was concerned in it, will grant. Now, without undertaking to express a belief that when many young men meet together all will or should be members of the Temperance Society, and not forgetting that to the natural ebullition of animal spirits on such an occasion some license may be allowed, as it certainly will be taken, still we cannot but protest against such behavior as was shown at Worcester, on the two grounds of the advantage and the honor of the students; *the advantage*, for outsiders, not ever inclined to be over-lenient to such a class, and experiencing a personal offense in such proceedings, are led to form their opinion of college manners and morality from this single exhibition; and when once this opinion is formed they do not hesitate to publicly express it, to the great injury of the reputation of the college, and to the great diminution of the possible repetition of such gatherings as were the cause of the offense. Moreover, this lawless behavior is to the dishonor of the students, as it directly casts upon them the imputation that public drunkenness is a necessary concomitant of public enjoyment, and a neglect of a decent respect for the comfort and the laws of the city that receives them the consequence of a permitted increase of their freedom of intercourse. In brief, while we believe that these troubles were the result of thoughtlessness rather than of deliberate malice, and consequently have perhaps received too harsh a treatment in some of the papers, it is clear, on the other hand, that, if the gentlemanly feeling and the morality of the collegians does not suffice to stop a repetition of the trouble, expediency tells them that continuance in such ways insures inevitably the interference of the authorities and the speedy stopping of the cause of the offense.

7. Book Notices

1. *The History of England, from the Accession of James II.* By Thomas Babington Macaulay. 4 vols. Small 8vo.
2. *The Works of* Charles Lamb. New Edition. 4 vols. Small 8vo.
3. *The Lives of Dr. John Donne, Sir Henry Wotton, Richard Hooker, George Herbert, and Dr. Robert Sanderson.* By Izaak Walton; with some Account of the Author and his Writings, by Thomas Zouch, D.D., F.L.S., Prebendary of Durham. New Edition, with Illustrative Notes, complete in One Volume. Small 8vo. Boston: Crosby, Nichols, Lee, & Co. For sale by Sever and Francis.

The first of the above-mentioned works is offered in a most respectable library form; four volumes, well bound, and legibly printed on good paper; and thus makes decidedly the most attractive edition of the History yet published in America, and almost the only one worthy of Lord Macaulay's fame. Of the work itself, so often criticized, and surviving criticism so well, there is nothing to be said here, except that it is one of those books which maturity admires, and even youth finds attractive, in spite of the early imbibed and righteous horror of history-books as such.

But while these volumes preserve in their aspect a kind of middle-aged sobriety, becoming to the gravity of their matter, the next quaternity appears with somewhat gayer air; here there is more open and larger type, a rambling generosity befitting the kind-hearted author. Leaving out of question some private leanings, and a silent preference to have Charles Lamb in a more tatterdemalion guise than the usual full-dress suit, just as he affected old copies of his favorite authors, with the odor of a dead century in their pages; we welcome this new edition as one of that order of publications which have done so much, within a few years, toward putting the better products of our press more nearly on a level with the best English work. The Life and Letters and Talfourd's Final Memorials, combined with the more familiar Essays of Elia, the Poems, and Lamb's Miscellaneous Works, are here brought together to make an edition most satisfactorily complete.

If we may say so, *Lamb* is rather a pungent flavor than solid food, he has that unmistakable individual *smack* which is a sure mark of genius, even when its existence in excess points, as in his case, to consequent limitations of scope. His criticisms, so frequently praised with too general a commendation, though always that of a connoisseur and lover of picturesque antiquity, are often biassed by his strong idiosyncrasies and personal preferences, for the very reason that he was so individual a man. Yet this, as well as his more creative work, is dear to us, for all belonged to one who had not only wit, but humor,—wit and love,—to a lovely spirit and a courageous heart.

But we must pass to the last volume on our list, the "Lives" of Izaak Walton.

This is the best edition of the book, and of the form in which it is issued we need only say it is of a size and appearance uniform with that of Lamb's Works, published by the same well-known firm. These "Lives," less known than Walton's charming pastoral, "The Complete Angler," make a book most opportune for our times; if, in an age of fast living, of hurrying business, and of unrepose, where the general taste is for condiments and dishes unnaturally stimulant, we had constantly on hand some works of this stamp, it might prove a wholesome corrective and a useful change of diet. There is here such a delightful old-world calm, a leisure so grave and saintly, that we feel on each page the effects of the holy life that fitted Walton for his task. Though it is vain enough to attempt to transplant the habits or modes of thought belonging to another period into this, still we may learn some purity of heart, and some tranquillity of spirit from these lives, which were first published, and found "passable, in an eloquent and captious age."

8. Book Notices

Marion Graham; or, "Higher than Happiness." By Meta Lander. Small 8vo. Boston: Crosby, Nichols, Lee, & Co.

We are sorry that the publishers, whose well-known names appear on the title-page of this book, should have so far fallen away from their usually careful selection as to have undertaken its publication. It belongs to that class of vulgar novels, and, what is worse, vulgar novels written by women, which are one of the afflictions of our day. Not that this story is of the worst or weakest order, but simply that it is irretrievably vulgar without displaying ability enough to excuse its printing. The plot is poor and unpleasing, and you cannot help feeling all the time about the characters that you know them better than the authoress does, and that they are neither handsome nor wise, in spite of her assurance to the contrary. The heroine, Marion, is introduced, at first, under the influence of a sort of preliminary passion for a Mr. Maynard, a minister (ministers are as thick throughout the book as salamanders after a rain; a new one creeps our from under every leaf we turn over). But Maynard, having foolishly preferred her friend, who is more spooney than herself, Marion gives up No. 1. Then enter a dark man, black hair, glittering teeth, eyes, voice, brain, everything, and Marion proceeds to increase the size of the volume that tells her life, with her passion for him, and extracts from the more familiar writings of Carlyle. But alas! he is an unbeliever, and she "renounces" him. So after knavish scenes with another handsome man, Mr. Perley, and other interesting by-play, she espouses No. 3 (Mr. Sunderland, a minister). Briefly after marriage enter No. 2 (who is now converted and a minister). Tableau. Marion gets over it, however, loves her husband well enough; husband and previous lover swear eternal friendship, and then the lover goes among the heathen. Now in all this there is a certain purity of tone that is really much better than the hot, bad atmosphere of some books of more ability, but *three* times are rather too many for a heroine to love, and there is through the whole this tainting vulgarity. There is no better example of this than the scene between Maurice and Julia Whipple in the arbor (p. 60) which is simply insufferable.

9. Pre-Raphaelitism

Within a few years a body of young men have stood forth in direct hostility to almost all the principles of modern art, and have attempted to restore by revolution the aims and motives of the painters of four hundred years ago. As if eager to provoke the contest which they challenge, they have signified their ambitious purpose by the name which they have themselves adopted,—the Pre-Raphaelites,—and hinted also at the principles which must insure their ultimate victory or defeat.

The belief on which the school founds its name is, that there exists a difference in kind between the spirit of the earlier painters, down to the time of Raphael, and those who have come after him. The difference consists in nothing less than this: that the first painted sincere and simple pictures,—the combined result of their limited technical knowledge, and their childlike religious faith,—whereas their successors painted pictures that were very often neither simple nor sincere. That such should have been the fact is quite conceivable, without imputing a personal responsibility to the later schools. Painting had advanced from its earliest stages of ignorance and conventionality, and consequently composition, drawing, and the other technical excellences of the art, as such, had acquired an undue preponderance over the spirit by which that art was prompted. In religion, too, the stage of infancy, which takes for granted all which it is told, had given way to the inquiring doubts of youth, and thus again the simplicity of the childlike work was gone forever.

The object of the Pre-Raphaelites is a reform in the spirit of their art, and a restoring of that spirit to its proper supremacy over the academic rules. The simplicity which comes from ignorance of the capacities of an art, or the religious credulity belonging to semibarbarism, of course cannot be restored; but religious devotion after the different light of our time may be, and still more is that deep sincerity which forms the only possible basis for noble work possible for all ages and for all religions. Pre-Raphaelitism, then, though to a degree a religious movement, professes chiefly to reform the spirit of art by making it more sincere.

As the proper means of attaining their object, the men of this school adopted, as their sole principle, *truth*. Truth, literal and uncompromising, in everything, from the first general conception down to the minutest detail of the finished work. When a Pre-Raphaelite conceives a composition, his aim is to think what would most probably have happened in fact, not what might have happened most picturesquely; and when he has his general plan clearly in his mind, he strives to work it out with the most faithful portraiture of which he is capable. The trees in the distance are drawn in the open air from real trees, the flowers of the foreground are painted from real flowers, the man is a friend of the painter, the woman may be his wife, and the infant his child.

Knowing what is the principle which the Pre-Raphaelites profess, we are naturally led to ask whether they have carried out their theory in their works. The answer is doubtful, to say the least. While their keen study of minute details gives them a nearly unequalled power in the delineation of delicate shades of expression and human feeling, they are, as a body, guilty of absurdities which it is equally hard to palliate or deny. We could excuse awkwardness and want of grace in a school which began by seeking truth and leaving beauty to come after as best it might. But when one of them makes the head of a man standing on the ground to be nearly level with that of a woman upon the top of a stile three feet high, we cannot call it awkwardness, but simply gross bad drawing,—deficiency in the very point where these artists should be strong. Whether the Pre-Raphaelite designs in general *are* probable, as they certainly are far from graceful, may well be questioned; certainly an attempt to imitate the position of the figures of the Huguenots,[56] which is one of their best and most widely known productions, will show how nearly impossible it is. Yet the pale, beseeching face of the woman in that picture shows a power unequalled in its way by the artists of any other modern school.

The brief statement of Pre-Raphaelitism is, that it is a reaction from the artificiality of earlier schools, and professedly a return to the simple copying of Nature. But as Art involves in its very nature *selection*, and as this school does not recognize that principle, the nature of its excellence and its failings becomes evident at once. Its pictures continually touch our hearts by their artless directness of appeal, and yet they are wanting in all those excellences of composition and arrangement, which are the fair and rightful field for the painter's genius. As painting had before this revival degenerated into merely academical study, so we may doubt whether the present works have a right to be called the fruits of art in its highest sense at all; but they are a step towards the truth; and when, in part by their means, a more careful study of Nature shall have become universal, we may hope that a later and maturer race of painters shall combine the highest art with the noblest truth, in works of worthy brotherhood with the greatest of all time.

---

[56]Sir John Everett Millais, *The Huguenot Lovers* (painting, 1852). This popular work was widely known through engravings. *See* [Anon.], *Naturalism & Genius*, *The New Path* (Oct. 1863) (periodical of American Pre-Raphaelites), *quoted in* Ferber, *"Determined Realists": The American Pre-Raphaelites and the Association for the Advancement of Truth in Art*, in *The New Path: Ruskin and the American Pre-Raphaelites* 25 (L. Ferber & W. Gerdts eds. 1985). The painting depicts two lovers, embracing, and the man's arms and woman's hips are awkwardly arranged. Ruskin praised the work as evidence of a new poetic art. 3 J. Ruskin, *Modern Painters* (1856), in 5 *The Works of John Ruskin, The Stones of Venice* (1853).

B. Spurious Work

Book Notices[57]

Autobiography of the Rev. Dr. Alexander Carlyle, *Minister of Inveresk, containing Memorials of the Men and Events of his Time*. Boston: Ticknor and Fields. 1861. 8vo. pp. 471.

It is very hard to forgive an artist who botches your pet heroes and heroines on paper or on canvas. He is himself a hero who is always ready to compare notes between his imagination and the *del. et sculp.* of Tom, Dick, or Harry, R.A. But, happily, such creatures are rare. Every sensible man wants Mendelssohn's "Songs without Words," *without* words, and Hans Christian Andersen's "Picturebook without Pictures," *without* illustrations. And these remarks are pertinent to the book in hand, because there is an irrepressible conflict between the portrait on steel at the beginning, and the portrait drawn on every page of the autobiography. Unfortunately, we are not aggrieved in this case, because the artist has fallen short of our conception, but rather because he appears a prodigious flatterer; so that we doubt if there be any one who is not disappointed (whether favorably or unfavorably) laying down the book.

Indeed, the spiritual face which serves for a frontispiece is wholly unsuggestive of the character or disposition of the man behind it. He is revealed to us in his autobiography as one who loved his stomach better than all earthly things, hardly wife and friends excepted; as one, the eras in whose life were determined by suppers, and the hardships by inferior fare; who in his eightieth year, could recall, and took pains to jot down, the quality and the kind of liquor which he drank on all the more or less important occasions in his experience; who remembers his claret, if he forgets all other incidents; and who mentions, with the utmost nonchalance, or even with reprehension, the fate of many an unfortunate boon-companion who fell victim to the bottle that was so attractive to himself. In his epitaph, which, like most men's, is not worth much, is recorded, "He too was worthy of the times." To our mind, nothing could be more gratuitous or unsupported by fact. He worthy of the times, who could depict the awful state of society in which he lived, and moved, and was a leading figure, without a single moral reflection, or a single indication that he lifted a finger to improve it? He drank with the hardest; ate with the greediest; thought a man squeamish who would not game for the payment of reckoning; for aught we can tell, was licentious, in his

---

[57]One source attributed this work to Holmes, but it may have been written by Garrison or by Holmes and Garrison jointly. *See supra* note 4.

younger days at least; never lisped of the immorality of war,—nay, took up arms himself, after having determined to become a follower of the Prince of Peace; and in short, was what other men were in those times,—as though the office of the Christian ministry were simply to follow, and not to lead.

There are two things of which Americans have no idea, in respect to Scotland; first the desperate condition of its people in the matter of drinking, and second, the intolerant bigotry of its Church. How much Dr. Carlyle did to ameliorate the former may be inferred from what has been already said. As for the latter, he seems to have been but a priest, who, not without pretensions to liberality, was zealous chiefly in adding to the privileges and emoluments of the clergy, and whose very liberality appears to have consisted in efforts to free his cloth from the responsibility attaching to its examples. For, take the Minister of Inveresk for all in all, it can only be said that he was what he himself loved not a little,—a jolly companion, whether at a tavern, a theatre, or a ball. The reader may well ask himself, in view of the premature death of all Carlyle's little ones,—"Who did sin, this man or his parents," that these died before their time?

Come we now to the book. It is the marvelous work of a gossiping memory, which retains even the most trivial circumstances of an eventful lifetime, and airs them for very wantonness. There are a thousand and one names to be met with, which an American cares not a chip about,—which makes the book, in some parts, very dull reading; but there are also many anecdotes and descriptions of really distinguished men, which, together with Carlyle's own adventures and personal history, render the whole entertaining enough. Hume, Garrick, Blair, Home, Robertson, Adam Smith, Ferguson, Smollett; Lords Chatham, Bute, and North; Dr. Franklin, etc., all enter as living characters upon the scene, and much interesting matter is written about them. Beyond this, the instructiveness of the work lies mostly in its revelations of the state of society at that day, and, on this account, we could wish that every one who believes in a Golden Age, whether in the garden of Eden, or among the Apennines, would read the Autobiography.

APPENDIX B

Translation of Greek Prize Essay by Robert Stoddart

Translator's Preface

THIS TRANSLATION is as close to Holmes's Greek as it can be while remaining English. I have added a few words [in square brackets] to clarify the syntax.

I have also reproduced all legible marks that appear in the essay. Holmes himself added references to Thucydides; Xenophon's *Cyropaedeia* and *Memorabilia*; and Plato's *Laws*, *Republic*, and *Timaeus*—probably to support usages that he considered odd (e.g., "magistracies" for "magistrates"). At the bottom of his first page, Holmes wrote a note introduced by an asterisk, "I had to guess at this accent. Word not in L&S [Liddell and Scott's *Greek Lexicon*]." No asterisk appears in the text. On the bottom of his third page, he wrote another note, introduced by an asterisk, referring to *hegemonia* (which I translate as "leadership"). The note suggests a synonym (*kyros*), but quickly becomes illegible.

The judge(s) of the essay competition underlined certain words for errors in spelling, accent, or meaning. (For example, Cyrus was not a satrap.) I cannot claim to understand all their objections, but have *italicized* the corresponding English words.

The prose style is rhetorical. Holmes seems to have enjoyed writing balanced, antithetical clauses sharpened with irony. A good example appears in the discussion of the Athenian debacle in Sicily: "After first helping as an advisor. . . ." To appreciate the grim humor, the reader must know that Nicias was the Athenian commander-in-chief.

No one but the author's blood relatives or Greek professors could read a prize essay for pleasure. This essay does show, however, that the young Holmes had mastered Greek grammar, appreciated Greek prose style, could compress a mass of facts into an argument, and could think and write clearly, even in a dead language.

Holmes's Essay

R:L.S. Senior Class

A coded message was sent by the magistrates (Thuc. 4.15) in Lacedaemon*ia* to Lysander in Asia, to order him to bring about the death of Alcibiades. Lysander accordingly mentioned this command (Plat. Leges 722) to Pharnabazus and asked him to carry it out, for Alcibiades was living in his [Pharnabazus's] satrapy at the time.

It is clear from the entire character of Pharnabazus that he would never have done such a thing to a man who was his guest had he not been forced by others much against his will—especially since he might easily have privily overlooked the escape of one who was doomed to die [anyway]. From these [considerations] we can clearly know that Cyrus discovered what Alcibiades was about to reveal and had ordered Pharnabazus to do what Lysander requested—and that what both these men commanded was too dangerous for him to shirk, much less to flout.

Pharnabazus accordingly sent his brother Magaios and his uncle Sisamithres with a command of hoplites to kill Alcibiades in the village in Phrygia where he was living. These men, not daring to enter his house by force, encircled it and set fire to it. Alcibiades, after having tried (Rep. 519B. Xen. Cyr. 1.6.22) to put out the fire, rushed against the attackers with a dagger in his right hand and a cloak wrapped around his left as a shield. No one dared to approach him. Rather, they threw a large number of spears and darts until he died—even though he had neither a shield nor any armor (Plato Tim 24B & Xen.) for protection. The *courtesan* with whom he was living, Timandra, wrapped her own cloaks around the body and performed all the customary rites.

Such was the crime that Cyrus and the Lacedaemonians did not hesitate to command, that the uncle and brother of a Persian satrap [did not hesitate] to commit—[a crime] by which this famous Athenian died before reaching his fiftieth year. Had he survived (Thuc. 4.27), there is no doubt that he would have accomplished something outstanding—for neither his nature nor his talent would have permitted him to remain at peace—but whether [he would have accomplished it] for the benefit of Athens is more doubtful. It is clear that if we regard the entire life of Alcibiades, he will seem not to have benefitted it [Athens] in comparison to (Xen. Cyr. 8.6.11) the much greater harm [he caused it].

More than any other *individual* he was responsible for the disastrous expedition to Sicily, although the expedition could not properly be called the work of any individual, but rather [should be said] to have arisen from a collective impulse. After first helping as an advisor, more than any other man, to drive the Athenians into this mad adventure (Thuc. VI. 54), he then as an exile helped, more than any other man but Nicias, to destroy the expedition and to turn the results into an even greater disaster. If not for him, Gylippus would never have been sent to Syracuse, Deceleia would not have been *fortified*, Chios and Miletus would not have revolted, and the conspiracy of the oligarchs would never have taken power.

Nor could anyone say that the three previous years turned out favorably for his country—[years] during which Alcibiades directed state affairs as leader of the Athenians—even in the matters that he himself managed, in the alliance with *Argos* and in the campaigns in the Peloponnesus. On the contrary, by advancing against the enemies to repel them when he had hardly been armed sufficiently, he gave the Lacedaemonians the opportunity to restore their damaged reputation and their leadership* through the great victory of *Mantinea*.

The part of the life of Alcibiades that was truly useful to his country and that truly brought him honor was the three years *ending* in his return from exile to Athens, in the second year of the *ninety-*third Olympiad.

What might have resulted from these three fortunate *years* was undone by the unexpected arrival of the *satrap* Cyrus. But in this very crisis, when Alcibiades should have applied even greater manliness (Thuc. 2.42) to accomplish his undertakings in the face of this new hindrance—in that crisis we find him pampered by (Xen. Memo. 1.2.24–5) the Athenians (who had just now unexpectedly welcomed him back) and wretchedly (Dem. [?] 142.18) lacking in the *earlier* virtue *by which* he had gained the welcome.

When we turn from his deeds to his character, goals, and methods, the chronicles of the Greeks will show few men worthy of *less* account, whether we consider him as he directed politics or as he *conducted* his own affairs. His goals were those of unbounded pride and vanity. His methods were rapacious and headstrong from the dealings he first had with Lacedaemonia and the Lacedaemonian elders until the end of his life. The devices by which his political enemies brought about his exile the first time were truly very shameful and unjust. But one *must* remember that if his enemies were more numerous and more dangerous than those of any other politician in Athens, the seed was sown by his own arrogance and contempt for the bounds of custom and society.

Nevertheless, Alcibiades was never defeated, by land or by sea. He never lacked for bravery, talent, daring, and power in *taking advantage of* new companions and new opportunities. His natural gifts and, in addition, his noble birth, wealth, and accomplishments sufficed to make him the first man in any government to which *he attached himself, whether* [it was the government] of the Athenians, the Lacedaemonians, *or* the Persians—an oligarchy, or a democracy. But he never inspired complete confidence in any of them; they all in a measure rejected him. In sum, we shall find few men in whom great power to act and to command was so completely blighted by bad character as [it was] in Alcibiades.

APPENDIX C

Selection from the Apology of Socrates[1]

(XXXIX) AS you are unwilling to wait a very little while, Athenians, you will soon have the reproach cast upon you by those who like to speak ill of our city, of having put to death Socrates, a wise man; for they will call me wise, though I am not, from their wish to throw shame upon you. Now if you had only shown a little patience, the thing you desire would have come to pass of itself; for you see my age; that I am now far advanced in years and that death is near at hand.—This I do not say to all of you but to those only who have voted for my condemnation (xxxi). [***] For to those of you on the other hand who have voted for my acquittal I would gladly speak of what has just taken place, while the Judges[2] are not yet ready, and the time has not quite come for me to go to the place where I must die.—For these few moments then, I beg of you to stay by me, since nothing hinders our talking with one another, while there is yet time, and I should like to tell you[3] the meaning of what has happened. The prophetic voice of my spiritual guide has heretofore never failed to oppose me, and in the most trifling matters, too, if I were about in any way to do otherwise than well. But now there has happened to me what by popular opinion is judged the greatest of all evils. Yet neither this morning as I left my house, nor as I was coming before the court, nor in any part of my speech did the spirit offer me the least opposition, and that, too, though it has often restrained me when speaking on other occasions. In this matter it has not restrained me in anything I have either said or done. What then is the reason of this? I will tell you. It proves that this is a good thing which has happened to me and that those who think that death is an evil do not judge at all rightly. [***] You then, my Judges, should feel high hopes with regard to death and hold this one thing firm in your convictions: that to a good man no event, whether he lives or dies, is evil, nor are his concerns ever neglected by the gods. My present condition is not the result of chance, but I plainly see that it was better for me to die and be freed

---

[1]From *Apology* 38c-d, 39e–40b, 41c–42a. Holmes's autograph manuscript is located at the Harvard University Archives.

[2]A correction on the manuscript in another hand replaces "Judges" with "officers."

[3]Inserted here in the manuscript in another hand is the phrase "as my friends."

from earthly care. On this account it is that no warning has turned me from my course and that I feel no anger either towards those who have condemned me or towards my accusers.—But I beg this of you, when my sons grow up, do you punish them and discipline them just as I have troubled you, should they seem to care for riches or anything else more than virtue, and if they being of no real account should think themselves something, rebuke them, as I too have you, for not attending to their proper business and for their too great self-esteem. If you do this, both I and my sons will have received the proper treatment at your hands. But now it is time for us to separate, for me to die and for you to live. Which is the better fate is unknown to all but God.

APPENDIX D

Contextual Chronology[1]

1841	Born Boston, March 8.
	Cooper, *The Deerslayer* (1841).
	Dvorak, born 1841.
	Morton uses ether as anesthesia, 1846.
	Marx and Engels, *The Communist Manifesto* (1846).
	Hawthorne, *The House of the Seven Gables* (1851).
	Whitman, *Leaves of Grass* (1855).
1857–61	Attends Harvard College.
	Holmes's father, *The Autocrat of the Breakfast Table* (1858).
	Darwin, *On the Origin of Species* (1859).
1861	Enlists (April), receives commission (July), and wounded (October) in Virginia.
1862	Wounded (September) in Maryland.
1863	Wounded (May) in Virginia.
	Pasteur pasteurizes wine, 1864.
1864–66	Attends Harvard Law School.
1867	Admitted to Massachusetts Bar.
1872	Marries Fanny Dixwell.
	Twain, *Tom Sawyer* (1875).
	Brahms Symphony no. 1 (1876).
1880	Publishes *The Common Law* (1881).
	Gilbert and Sullivan, "The Pirates of Penzance" (1880).
1882	Professor at Harvard Law School.

[1]For more traditional and complete biographical chronologies, *see* G. Aichele, *Oliver Wendell Holmes: Soldier, Scholar, Judge* 167–71 (1989); 2 M. Howe, *Justice Oliver Wendell Holmes: The Proving Years* 1870–1882 285–86 (1963); S. Novick, *Honorable Justice: The Life of Oliver Wendell Holmes* 379–82 (1989).

1883	Appointed justice of Massachusetts Supreme Judicial Court.
1894	Publishes *Privilege, Malice and Intent.*
1897	Delivers "The Path of the Law."
1899	Delivers "Law in Science and Science in Law."
	Freud, *On the Interpretation of Dreams* (1899).
	Planck discovers quantum mechanics, 1900.
1902	Appointed to Supreme Court and moves to Washington, D.C.
	Einstein's Special Theory of Relativity, 1905.
	Stravinsky, *Rite of Spring* (1913).
	Russian Revolution, 1917.
1920	Publishes *Collected Legal Papers* (1921), collecting work from 1885 to 1918.
	Joyce, *Ulysses* (1922).
	Mann, *The Magic Mountain* (1924).
	Scopes Monkey Trial, 1925.
1929	Wife dies.
1932	Resigns from Court.
	Nazi seizure of power, 1933.
	F.D.R. president, 1933.
1935	Dies, Washington, D.C., March 6.
	Gershwin, "Porgy and Bess" (1935).
	Sulfa drugs, 1935.

Table of Cases

Abrams v. United States, 250 U.S. 616 (1919), 4n.7

American Banana Co. v. United Fruit Co., 213 U.S. 347 (1909), 13n.45

Black and White Taxicab & Transfer Co. v. Brown & Yellow Taxicab & Transfer Co., 276 U.S. 518 (1928), 18n.62, 85n.111

Buck v. Bell, 274 U.S. 200 (1927), 4n.8

Comegys v. Vasse, 26 U.S. (1 Pet. 193) 108 (1828), 21n.72

Erie Railroad Co. v. Tompkins, 304 U.S. 64 (1937), 17-18n.62, 93

Fountleroy v. Lum, 210 U.S. 120 (1908), 26n.84

Gitlow v. New York, 268 U.S. 652 (1925), 4n.5

Heard v. Sturgis, 146 Mass. 545 (1888), *reversed sub nom. Williams v. Heard*, 140 U.S. 529 (1891), 19-26, 92

Kenney v. Supreme Lodge of the World, 252 U.S. 411 (1920), 26n.84

Lochner v. New York, 198 U.S. 45 (1905), 4n.9

Southern Pacific Co. v. Jensen, 244 U.S. 205 (1917), 85n.113

Swift v. Tyson, 41 U.S. (16 Pet.) 1 (1842), 18n.62

Index

Note: This index does not cover the writings by Holmes that are published as appendices, but it does include the introductions and annotations to those appendices.